Waiting for Life:
A Cancer Survivor's Story of Death, Humor, and Love

by
Daniel A. Seda, Ph.D.

Author's Note

The hardest part of sharing my story was finding the courage and determination to set it all down on paper with what seemed like lifetimes of experiences to choose from. Seeing so much of oneself in written form can be a terrifying ordeal, to say the least. Luckily, I've lived a colorful life; so, fear isn't as much of a motivating factor as it would be for others to remain silent for very long.

It was 2021, when I finally decided to collect my writings from old journals and bind them into a publishable manuscript. Little did I know that my healing journey over the past three decades would one day find its way into your hands. It's my hope that this expansive look at my innermost struggles and triumphs can help others, such as yourself, find the courage to keep going, even when the most available option may be anything but survival.

If you're reading this now, then I pray you find within these pages something useful, hilarious, and inspiring. Thank you for sharing your journey with me!

"The people who are most successful at living and loving are those who can learn to wait successfully."
– Melody Beattie –

Table of Contents

Preparation for the Big Day

We were anticipating the big day as we huddled by the entryway of our new home, expecting the best but planning for the worst. Staring down the hallway, it was clear that our four-year vision--to own a home in the heart of San Francisco--was not going to come to fruition the way we had planned it. What we had now, was ground zero for event planning and operations. It had been a long time coming, but I hadn't been fully present enough to experience it all because of the success of my business and managing all the family drama in the weeks leading up to our pending nuptials.

Bryan stepped across the threshold of our apartment in the city, pushing aside stacks of envelopes on his way into the foyer. He was obviously agitated at the mess scattered all over the floor since our impromptu excursion to Europe. "I just want to come home from a nice vacation and not have to clean up anything," he declared.

I shrugged my shoulders and wiped sweat from my brow. Bryan smiled quietly, closed the door behind him, and flicked on the hall light to reveal stacks of boxes, decorations, and linens reaching almost to the top of the ceiling and spilling over onto the hallway rug. There was little I could do but laugh to myself while Bryan toiled and grimaced picking up more stray invitations off the floor in counterprotest.

I looked at Bryan and spoke with a calm tone: "It'll be alright, honey. You don't have to worry so much. I'll be there with you. We're in this together. Remember, it's one-two-three, one-two-three. Ok?" I mimed the movements of a waltz, recalling the dance classes we took years prior in preparation for the reception. I still couldn't believe how much progress Bryan had made in such a short amount of time. Of course, it had been well over a year of lessons, but sometimes it takes longer for some people to master skills that don't come as naturally to them as they do to others.

I bumped up the volume of my voice as we danced to an imaginary orchestra. "One-two-three, one-two-three, one-two-three…" Bryan tried to follow but he was fumbling on the two and eventually stopped having fun all together.

"One-two-three, one-two-one…God! I can't do this! Can we change songs or something? Why can't we have our first dance to something like techno?" Bryan asked impatiently.

I methodically grabbed his face in my hand with a gentle caress. I brushed Bryan's forehead to expose his tanned, oily skin.

"Honey, it's just a wedding. People have them all the time. And it's just one dance. You can do it. I've seen you practicing. Just trust yourself. I'll be there with you every step of the way," I said.

"You saw me practicing? When?" Bryan became easily annoyed and confrontational when he thought his private moments were being scrutinized.

"When you got up to stretch from the computer last week. I was in the kitchen making lunch. I saw you get up and start dancing. It was sweet."

"No, I didn't. You didn't see me…"

"Honey, I see a lot of things people don't. I hear a lot of things people can't. I can tell you that you were petting Charlie and had him on his hind legs and you two were dancing to a sweet, swinging melody playing in your head. You didn't think anyone was around, but I was happy to see you being so sweet with Charlie. It makes my heart smile when you do things like that and don't expect anyone else to be noticing."

Bryan smiled knowingly and finally rested in my wistful gaze. We shared a brief kiss and started dancing again. This time, Bryan let go and started listening to a steady beat in his ears. A slight smile appeared through Bryan's pursed lips as we both looked at each other with a warm-hearted glow.

And just like that, we retreated upstairs to revel in the moments of bliss before the wedding madness the only way we knew how.

We arrived in Asheville the following day to prepare for the big event. It was a hot late-May morning and there was much to do before everyone else arrived.

Bryan poked around trying to make some sense of the chaos, stepping over flower arrangements and cummerbunds; looking for some sense of order to invest his sanity in.

"Babe, where should I put this?" Bryan offered me a box from behind the sitting chair. "It looks like it has a bunch of photos and knickknacks. I'll just go put it upstairs with the rest of your stuff."

I peered out from under a stack of old wedding invitations and grabbed the box from Bryan's hands. Thinking hard to myself about its contents.

"Hold on. That looks familiar." I immediately started digging, intrigued at the contents.

With my head practically inside the box, I echoed, "I think this is from my old childhood room back at my parent's place. Where did you get this?"

"I found it by the chair. I was gonna put it upstairs. Do you want to keep it?"

I pulled out a toy car and a swimming ribbon, "You see, babe, there was a time I did do manly things. Oh, and look…the painting I made in kindergarten where I painted myself with six fingers! Can you believe it?"

"Yes, I can, honey." He said with an underwhelmed smirk.

"Oh, stop it, Bryan." I motioned him to keep shuffling.

"What's this?" Bryan pulled out a heavy book wrapped in leather binding with a thin braid tying the papyrus pages together. My eyes widened.

"That's my journal!" I grabbed it gleefully from Bryan's hardened hands and held it directly in front of me transfixed by all the weathered details. "You found it! I've been looking for this for years. I can't believe you found it!"

"Well, honey, you really have to remember where you put things. We could end up losing our marriage license like that, you know?"

"Oh, honey, stop it." I flippantly motioned to Bryan to take it upstairs to our bedroom.

"Can you please put it upstairs by my end table? I don't want to lose it again. You're never going to believe what's in that book. It's all my most ridiculous stories and the crazy adventures that I've written down for decades. One of these days I'm going to put it in a book. You'll see. Can you put this box upstairs for me, please?" I looked at Bryan with puppy dog eyes holding my newfound treasure in the tips of my hands.

Bryan took the box from my hands with a knowing grin. "If you weren't so adorable, I would think you were trying to avoid going up another flight of stairs."

"Well, it's hot and there's so many damn hills in San Francisco. Please, honey. I've gotta find the invoice for the caterers. I have to cut them a check before they arrive at the hotel."

Bryan looked at me and huffed. He walked up the stairs sighing as I flitted off down the hallway to the dining room table to go through some additional paperwork.

"Right, blame it on the caterers," Bryan murmured as he begrudgingly took each heavy step up the stairs.

"I heard that!" I exclaimed from a few rooms away.

Our hotel was a majestic, old Victorian mansion from the late 1800s, properly restored to its former glory to make way for the patrons who would be wistfully served by the current yoga-loving retreat sanctuary staff.

I'd envisioned a place where people could gather and enjoy a gay wedding without it having to feel too overwhelming for our straight family and friends. Bryan wasn't too keen on the idea when he first heard about it, but through the years I convinced him that miracles can happen. He eventually decided to give it a shot.

I placed the book on the table next to a white binder where all the wedding paperwork was stored. I was nothing if not organized, even though my style of organization left a lot to be desired by technical pragmatists like Bryan. We both had a quirky way of handling each other's idiosyncrasies. We were happy if not constantly surprised and supported by each other in wonderful ways.

I opened the big, white binder and noticed old magazine clippings and online articles I had printed out to get ideas for the big day. There were ill-fated drawings, charts for table seating, and maps of cool things for the guests. I couldn't believe it was just about time for all the planning to finally come to fruition. It was almost too much to think about, and now it was all staring me right in the face.

I looked around the room at everything that had took place to get to this point; things that were once just a dream. There was a bookshelf of binders that held old scripts of musicals I'd been in and plays I had written as a teenager, and pages of music I'd gathered over the years that were now set aside to share with my music students when we got back to California. I walked over to the bookshelf and pulled out another binder. It was marked "Multiviewing" in a bright and colorful font. I smiled to myself knowing full well it was my first company and my first venture into the beginnings of a life's dream that was manifesting all around me.

I put the binder back on the shelf and made my way across the wall of the dining room. In front of a window, facing the street, a giant mirror hung a bit too lopsided for my taste. As I reached to adjust it, I saw myself in the mirror and stopped dead in my tracks. It had been a long time since I'd really taken a good look at myself in all my aging glory. I had been so busy creating our future that I hadn't had a lot of time to remember my past.

The years had become a little more visible than they were before, but still there was a soft glow about me that seemed relatively ethereal and ageless; a forever Peter Pan-like spirit that had survived an endless array of carefree days. But now I was thrilled to be starting a new chapter with the man that I loved.

I made my way back to the table and glanced down at my book. The leather was scratched and worn and the strap holding the bulging pages together was stretched taught. I moved my hands up and down the front cover remembering what it felt like to be so engrossed in my writings that the subway rides in New York City became the gleaming sandy beaches of the Caribbean. With a smile on my face, I remembered the taste of ackey and salt fish breakfasts at the Ritz Carlton in Mo' Bay, and the conversations I had with Phyllis along the way.

Suddenly, a flood of emotion came over me. I couldn't believe it had been so long since I'd graced the pages of this book that I once considered my sacred temple; the place I'd go to when all the walls around me were crumbling. I was nostalgic and sad, and a little surprised at how much time had passed without hardly a glance.

Most people never knew it, but it was writing that got me through the tough times. And there were many. When there was barely a glimmer of hope in sight, I at least had pages to go to to find comfort and peace. I could always turn another page and put my pen to paper or my fingers to the keyboard for just one more chapter or sentence. This process was my only constant, without exceptions or expectations, and I dearly needed that in my otherwise tattered life.

I took the book in my hands and turned it over to expose the back binding that had been sitting on the bottom of the box for too long. The leather backing had creases pressed into it--like it had been underneath heavy objects for too long--with the indentations to demarcate how often it had shifted in its time away from my care. I patted it on the back as if to awaken it from its hibernating slumber.

I delicately untied the leather knot with my chewed-down fingernails. Gathering the thick cover in between my left thumb and index finger, I unfurled my frenzied meanderings as if entering uncharted territory with the familiar exhilaration of coming home after a tumultuous voyage at sea. My strange affinity for recanting the details of these adventures lay meticulously carved into the pages with blue and black ink, as if to try and never forget any part of my journey for as long as I was able to carry it with me.

It was time to go back into my history to take a long hard look at how my life had changed over the course of the last three decades. Tomorrow I'd be a husband, with all the responsibilities, joys, and pains of dedicating my life to someone else in the hopes of creating a better one for the both of us. I opened the handwritten pages of my manuscript and began to read what time had almost forgotten.

Life as a Sick Kid

In preschool, I ate Play-Doh and climbed on dragons made of recycled tires and chains. We lived in New Jersey at the time, close to my uncle who later developed lung cancer: a consequence of asbestos and lead-based paints. At three, I was talking to birds and removing shiny objects from the garbage disposal with my bare hands. I guess that's why I never became an accountant like my father, too much tactile sensitivity. By four, I had gotten very sick for reasons no one knew and needed to be treated at Duke Children's Hospital in North Carolina, which was one of the best hospitals in the country for kids with cancer at the time. That's what brought our family down South.

Moving away from the city meant that my older brother Mike and I could no longer play the game of "Name That Smell" because dogs in the South had proper poopy etiquette unlike the North where pigeons and geese shit without shame. I wondered what life would be like in a place where nature wasn't limited to a government cheese box atop a windowsill, where budding flowers were more plentiful than potholes on the Verrazano, and where discarded parking tickets weren't blown by bus exhaust down Morris Park Avenue.

It was hard to imagine a world that was different from the gray skies of New Jersey or the gum-lined sidewalks of the Bronx. Still, that was the earliest I can remember feeling utterly safe in the world and free to dream without hesitancy or limitations. Like a victim of domestic abuse, I was going to have to find a way to thrive in wide open spaces even though everything inside me wanted to run back to the folded arms of chain-smoking Lady Liberty. At least there I wouldn't be forced to carry on ad nauseam conversations with total strangers because it was the "Southern thing to do."

The symptoms started in the backseat of dad's Dodge Dart. I developed a pain that was first thought of as a gas bubble but felt more like an atomic bomb about to explode in the pit of my stomach. All I had to do was find someone willing and able to pull my finger and all my worries would cease. With a last-ditch effort to seek relief, I sat clenching my stomach on the soft velvet seats, writhing in pain, and proceeded to dislocate my right pointer finger until eventually passing out from exhaustion.

I remembered how strong of a man my dad was, so I tried not to cry in front of him. My earliest memory of my father was watching him workout in the garage wearing a dingy white t-shirt with sweat beading from his tanned, receding hairline: a balding Bernardo from *Westside Story*. His high, ribbed tube socks and paint-stained burgundy sweatpants replaced his everyday business attire with the drawstring of his pants tied tight and high above his navel.

He was predictable for the most part--at least to me at that age. I always knew I'd be safe with him back then, even if the world came crashing down on us both because he had a natural knack for surviving anything amidst the harshest circumstances. There were times though when he frightened me with his temper; times when I saw hatred behind his tired eyes that I could not understand at the time. But at least he was there when he was, doing what he knew how to do to provide for his family the best way he could. We would hop on and off subway cars together, his briefcase in one hand and my small, delicate palm in the other.

My mother was a nurse and someone whose mental strength matched my dad's physical prowess. Although she considered Ibuprofen an appropriate treatment for an episodic embolism, she noticed something wasn't right when I complained of a bad pain in my tummy. She possessed the innate ability of knowing when things weren't right and was always prepared for the worst situations to occur at any given moment.

I don't recall what eventually took place at the hospital or the conversations they had in the examination room about my potential illness, but one thing was certain: no one was going to leave until someone supplied my mother with answers for fear of losing a desired appendage. Back then, the thought of curing anything remotely resembling cancer was a radical idea. But my mother was someone who was obstinate enough to remain convinced that her son was going to live even if that meant administering care with latex gloves instead of a warm embrace.

My symptoms were put into a computer and the possible treatments were chosen at random. There was a fifty/fifty chance I'd live or die. I guess the same went for the doctors as far as my mother was concerned.

She kept looking at me in the backseat from the rearview mirror and was so panicky in those moments before we got to the hospital that I was afraid of the repercussions my father would have faced if he had missed another exit on the expressway. Each bump in the road made every sharp pain in my stomach more piercing and my desperate need to quickly get to a doctor that much more urgent. It was a race against time, taxis, and stoplights. Somehow, it seemed that the faster we got there, the better everything would be, and life would go back to normal again. If there ever was such a thing.

"It's probably just gas, Annie," my father jokingly commented to ease the tension in the car, as he always tended to do in situations requiring adult decision-making.

My mother retorted, "Michael, does this look like constipation to you? Shut up and drive!"

In the backseat I had my hand on my stomach applying pressure to the tennis ball-sized lump that was growing angrily in my belly. I remember being tested for everything under the sun. Fluorescent-lit hallways with checkered white floors; and my gurney bumping open long, white doors with a frenzy of nurses and doctors hovering over me. The familiar odor of latex and the piercing sensation of needles being shoved deep into my tiny body would soon accompany strangers holding me down and asking me questions to get my mind off what was really happening.

I don't remember my father being around very much after that. I'd bet he would have wanted to be there to see his son get better every step of the way, but there was nothing he could do about the situation, which I'm sure frustrated him greatly. His child's fate rested in the hands of God and science and all he could do was work hard, make money to keep us afloat, and hope that his prayers would eventually be answered.

I never felt that he didn't love me during this difficult time in both of our lives, nor my mother for that matter. But I remember many times wondering where he was…where anyone was, honestly. Even at that age, I understood on some level the gravity of the situation and knew that if I showed how much the pain really hurt me that it would have made others around me feel helpless and sad because there was really nothing they could do but wait. So, I learned to endure pain in a way that not many children my age could comprehend for the sake of everyone else's emotional comfort.

Now, my mother's cooking was an entirely different story. She could read recipes and do her best to stick to them, but that creative bug would rear its ugly head and inspire her to throw in a lump of this and a few spoonfuls of that, ultimately destroying a once perfectly devised culinary design by an obvious professional. Regrettably, I too possess that gene, as Bryan would woefully attest. So, freeze-dried meatloaf, crunchy mashed potatoes, and watery Jell-O from the hospital cafeteria hardly fazed me one bit.

I never worried about not getting better. I was too young to "have to do" anything but survive. I just knew I wasn't supposed to die for a lot of difficult reasons that hardly had much to do with my own needs.

My mother used to say that the only time she heard my father cry was when she called to tell him that I had been diagnosed with Acute Lymphoblastic Leukemia. A story I've decided to believe for its beauty and simplicity, rather than for its factual premise; like old love stories that always end with a kiss, or when the hero in a movie seems all too perfect to be real.

Both of my parents grew up in tenement housing within the concrete jungles of the New York City projects, raised by parents who were penny-pinching children of the Depression. Life for them was a far cry from how I was raised: a child who would never starve due to the abundance of cheap, processed foods available for the middle class during the mid '80s and '90s. I would be given as many luxuries as my parents' labors and the power of high-interest credit cards would yield, even though these paled in comparison to the peaceful, united family I longed for. Somehow, we always made it, barely by the skin of our teeth.

By this time, we were already settled in our new place in Raleigh, North Carolina. I was four and was being treated at Duke Children's Hospital in Durham, which was about a half-an-hour putter away in our beige campervan with the dented hubcap and faded-blue racing streak on the side for added social embarrassment. It was the hottest summer on record, before the awareness of global warming would be pumped into mainstream media a decade or so later. All five of us slept together in the den of our home on Plateau Lane on a sandy-colored carpet like a family of suburban refugees awaiting trial and eminent deportation.

It was one of those lovely brown and white Tudor homes with matching shutters, triangular points on the roof tops, an orange and yellow stained-glass front door, and a lush Crepe Myrtle spilling over onto the driveway that bloomed every spring like clockwork. A slight hill on the side of our home divided the sidewalk and our lawn where my younger brother, Erik, and I would occasionally play soccer after school. Neighbors could see in the large windows to our living room from the street, and our fake Christmas tree would be on display each December until early June. Mom found work as a nurse at a convalescent center downtown and dad had to stay in New York for a while until our financial situation settled down.

I spent most of my time in and out of the hospital receiving chemo and radiation therapy, complete with regular blood tests and checkups. I must have had blood drawn from every vein in my body, been poked and prodded by innumerable sharp objects, and all the while the thought of death never entered my mind. I don't think my mother would have allowed such a thing. I wanted to show my mom that there was nothing to worry about; that her little soldier was going to pull through with flying colors. I learned a powerful technique of changing the energy in a room, as an emotional escape artist of sorts, when I knew my pain was surging beyond any reasonable threshold. It was no surprise that I ended up pursuing a career as a performer a decade later.

One time, my mom said that I jumped on a table after getting my blood drawn and danced around smiling just to make her and the nurses laugh. I'd sing into the stethoscope around my neck, make puppets out of tongue depressors and cotton swabs, let the other kids win at board games in the playroom, and cheered when the staff made turkeys out of inflated surgical gloves. All the while, secretly wishing I was somewhere less exhausting.

My mother told me stories about the times I flatlined that always left me spellbound. Of course, they never knew what I had experienced at the time, but it was nice to hear some validation during those life-altering moments. On one occasion, I had a seizure where nothing but the tip of my head and the bottom of my heels were touching the operating table and where packs of ice were pressed firmly into my armpits and groin to reduce my boiling fever. I wouldn't want to remember the overturned ambulance that almost killed me when I was being rushed to the emergency room one rainy night after a doctor misdiagnosed me and was afraid of being sued for medical malpractice.

For such a young kid, I do remember a lot back then. Spinal taps and painful blood tests were vividly seared into my memory no matter how much I wanted to forget them; the shooting pains down my legs from the student doctors' miscalculations of the proximity to my spinal nerve and the myriad of torturous contraptions the current medical field was toying with to draw blood at my expense. Sadly, I got used to being treated like a guinea pig, or a "pioneer for the latest medical advancements." I remember the odd sensation when the needles would enter my arms or legs and the cool, liquid feeling that would take over me when the chemicals began circulating through my bloodstream. I felt I had no control over my own body back then, but I knew it was just something I had to endure for everyone's sake.

I remember becoming frail and weak from the disease and the effects of all the new therapies being used on me at the time. I lost my hair and decided to wear a cap I got from a trip to Barnum and Baley's Circus. A head covering made going out in public a lot easier. My skin had turned snow white with a jaundiced tinge. My eyes sunk into my skull and dark circles began to appear underneath them like shadows of a little boy locked inside a monster with puffy cheeks, clearly showing the effects of experimental therapies and steroids.

"I got some news from the doctor today, Danny. Your white blood cell count is up!" My mother's mood would rarely perk up during moments where my prognosis seemed overwhelmingly hopeful.

I had just woken up to a squeaky table with a plastic tray of rubbery eggs, a gummy slice of white bread and a kid-sized carton of apple juice. I was too tired to smile at the good news. I hadn't noticed the first sprouts of gray in my mother's otherwise thick, black hair until a few moments after waking. She was so beautiful even in that oversized red Mickey Mouse sweatshirt, black stretch pants, and thick glasses she always wore to hide her weight.

For Christmas that year, Erik and I would play make-believe in the Christmas tree box that spent most of its days shoved into a corner of the attic. We'd dress the plastic tree with multi-colored lights and gold garland that was eventually shed all over the floor, eaten by the cats, but never fully digested. The litter box would glitter and glisten each December catching our cat off guard mid dig.

My younger brother was such a wonderful companion on our little trips to Neverland. Together we would conquer the world and save fair maidens from the evil clutches of monsters and sorcerers. I wanted to believe so badly that anything was possible; that there were no limits to the power of our imaginations. There were too many reasons why I should have died, and I got upset when people told me I couldn't do something because of my supposed handicaps. I was getting better, and no one could tell me I wasn't going to live every minute of my life to its fullest. I was as hard-headed as my mother, even at that age.

Much of the memories I have from my childhood come from a familiar smell. It was the odor of hospitals and convalescent centers, the smell of over-cleanliness and over-washed hands, of Betadine and Clorox on white lab coats and nurse's uniforms. Even the hospital food that I would affectionately call my "home-cooked meals" smelled of this antiseptic spray rinse left over from the mass disinfection process.

There was a playroom at the hospital. I'd see little boys and girls come and go, but one of them stayed the longest and became not only a friend but a teacher as well. This little boy at the hospital suffered from third-degree burns all over his body. We played blocks together and built tall buildings that could be quickly toppled over when our need to control something in our otherwise out-of-control lives overtook us.

It was when I never saw him again after those many months together that I was first introduced to the idea of death. It was the elephant in the room that loomed over our heads. Before that time, I had noticed--rather, I had grown accustomed to expecting--people entering and leaving my life without reason or question; often, never to return. The nurses and doctors walked in and out of my room like a working assembly line sticking me with various objects and telling me what a good boy I was. But I never saw that young boy again. His name still escapes me, but his bandaged body is etched in my memory, and my desire to help people like him remains a part of my life to this day.

Another young child entered my life that was deaf and had the same sort of cancer as me. Her mother taught me sign language and I used to walk into her room to study with her. She taught me to sign "apple" and "mother" and I went around signing what I had recently learned to all the nurses on the floor, half to make them smile and half to make myself feel something other than pitied. In fact, I still remember like it was second nature to me, because of the exhaustible times I signed to anyone who would give me a hint of recognition as to what being normal might look or feel like.

I went over to her room, Teddy Ruxpin bear in hand, as I had done a handful of times prior. I was approaching the doorway from the long hallway and there was a strange light around everyone as they huddled around her hospital bed. I thought she was sleeping, so I cautiously continued walking down the hall toward her just to see if anyone was playing a trick on me. As I came closer, a nurse called my name from the reception desk and I noticed she was preparing to chase after me. But something took over me, and I just had to keep walking toward the light.

I steadied my approach to the doorway and could see the girl's mother crying and holding her mouth as she looked at her daughter lying lifeless there on the bed. She glanced over at me for a split second. I stood motionless and confused, without a clue as to what I should do next. I was waiting for someone to say something, anything. The light got brighter around them the more I focused on the girl's body, and as quickly as the mother glanced at me, she turned her head to cry out of my sight and someone from inside quickly swung the door shut in front of me.

I was so angry. A part of me knew I'd never see her again and another part of me didn't know why it had to be that way. *Why was I any different? Why did I have to get Leukemia in the first place? Why am I stuck here when everyone else gets to leave and go home? Why can't I just get up out of bed and run around like every other little boy and girl my age, go to school, or play on a playground?* None of it made any sense to my young mind and there wasn't an adult in sight who could explain it to me. I was intimately aware of death at a very young age, and I had already experienced things that most children wouldn't have imagined in their worst nightmares. But there was an overwhelming sense that everything was going to be ok.

What are these stupid tubes and needles stuck inside my arm? What's this pole I have to lug around all the time? What did I, or any other kid here, do to deserve all this pain? What am I waiting around for; another test, another miracle, another day of this?

Enough was enough. I stormed into my room almost forgetting my I-V pole and tried to force myself to sleep by squeezing my eyes as tight as I could. If only I could fall asleep as fast as I wanted to, I'd be in a place where nothing could hurt me anymore or make me feel any different than anyone else. I wasn't just tired physically and emotionally, but I was tired of waiting for things to get better, not understanding any of it all, and tired of knowing too much about the realities of life with cancer at such a young age.

My Near-Death Experience

What I failed to understand at the time was that I already had a similar experience to the young girl in the hospital room, but rather than take my soul to a place where there was no more pain, I was kept alive for reasons I wouldn't comprehend until much later. This deep sense of knowing would show itself again in my early twenties after I was hit by a speeding taxi on Park Avenue. It's taken me almost four decades to finally put these pieces together.

You see, when I was growing up, I was--for lack of a better word--different. I could always remember so many more details and felt situations way deeper than most others I encountered. I had an effeminate way of approaching most situations, which was usually more concerned with relationships rather than things, so I felt quite foreign from the rest of the other boys. I never seemed to experience the world the same as those my age.

For me, the birds always chirped a little more chipper, the sun shined a whole lot brighter, violence on TV never got easier to handle, and conflicts with my family cut way too deep for me to bear. I always saw the big picture before I could see the little things, and it made dealing with practical, everyday matters relatively incomprehensible. Luckily, in academia I found satisfaction in the structure I was severely lacking at home. School allowed me to ask questions and seek the answers in a relatively safe environment--avoiding the devastating blows of most intimate and real-world interactions.

Now, I know I mentioned earlier about flatlining, where my heart stopped beating and my brain activity appeared to have ceased, and I don't remember the ambulance ride that had me lying dead in a ditch, but I do remember the time I was being operated on and had a near-death experience. Since I was a child, the simplicity of this encounter may have appeared to be inconsequential, but it eventually explained how I continued moving through life and the intense life-altering situations that transpired two decades later.

The challenge is that my family never wanted to talk about my bout with cancer. I was told by several family members that me having cancer ruined my family; that I was the cause of all the family's problems. If I didn't have cancer my father wouldn't have had to stay up North and work to keep the medical insurance and the house afloat. That would mean my mom wouldn't have been without a husband at home so often and would have somehow miraculously handled her chronic depression better. It would have meant that my older brother, who was a relentless bully to me during my formative years, wouldn't have been so messed up from the start because I apparently got too much attention from my parents during those two years while I was in the hospital. These are all explanations I was told by family members over the decades and these sentiments were instilled in me no matter what the truth really was. I wasn't supposed to talk about my experiences because it would make other people feel uncomfortable, angry, and sad.

So, I learned early on to stuff my emotions because no one would be able to understand them. How would I be able to express my emotions in a manner that could help other people understand? I wasn't given the language or guidance to do so from the start. This realization plagued me, and I eventually begged my parents for therapy, but my mother had bad experiences with psychiatrists in her family and never saw any positive effects from counseling. It was constantly reinforced that my feelings and experiences were not important to the people I was supposed to be closest to, so this fact drove me to seek alternative avenues to learn more about myself and my own soul's journey. Who knows if, in the end, this was a blessing or a curse?

There's a memory that has been yearning to be uncovered within my psyche since childhood. For the longest time, I didn't understand why this event was so important. I was maybe five years old, so my experiences then were relatively simplistic.

The situation was rather chaotic, yet there was a serenity at arm's length that I eventually tapped into once my consciousness was able to leave my physical body. I can't recall how much time it took because there was no concept of time where I was. Nothing was as important as the present moment and the person standing next to me. I knew it was important to eventually tell people my story so that if I died, I could at least have the chance to bring a deeper knowing of what lies beyond the veil to more people.

To my recollection, I had been taken to the emergency room and was unresponsive. I do not know how but this was where I remember watching myself from outside of my body. At this point, I was unconscious, but my soul had been freed from my physical body. I remember standing next to a very tall man in what seemed like a long, etheric robe. I remember knowing innately that I wasn't supposed to look at him. It wasn't a fear, but it had something to do with the knowing that if I saw him, I wouldn't want to stay on Earth.

I could feel him next to me, his tall stature, his emanating knowingness, and loving kindness he exuded by his mere presence. He was offering me the opportunity to witness truth in a way I had never experienced before from any other adult in my life at the time. He was protective, compassionate, and respectfully inquisitive in a healthy, open, humorous way. We both stood at what felt like maybe ten feet away from my body. My physical body was lying on the operating table and there was a flurry of nurses and doctors around me packing things under my appendages that were quickly becoming rigid and extended.

During this time that felt like an eternity, I remember it as merely moments. Everything was peaceful and I did not experience the chaos of any alarming sounds that would normally animate and ground one in their physical senses. It was almost as if the sound was turned off on a television and I was left watching a silent movie without any emotional attachment to what I was witnessing. The whole experience felt more like a peaceful science experiment, devoid of weighty human emotion, with a fascinating over-arching perspective, while simultaneously being able to pinpoint any thought or action from anywhere at a moment's whim.

Since I was so young, I did not have the natural propensions I do now where I would have wanted to ask more questions and seek more answers from the man next to me or to make more sense of the experiences I had witnessed. In those moments back then, I was safe and free from pain, and I knew more in those instantaneous minutes than I could have otherwise from a physiological perspective.

I don't remember holding hands with the man next to me. I just remember standing next to him and how big he felt. Then, I remember a natural curiosity come over me as I tried to see what the nurses were sticking in my crevices and all over me. I noticed small packs of ice that reminded me of Mr. Potato Head; a children's toys that you could attach appendages to and play with. In that moment, I began to remember how much I liked to play with those toys in the hospital playroom.

I started to smile a bit and thought about how much fun I used to have while playing with the other kids in the hospital. At that point, I saw my physical torso on the table rise up in the air as if I had been electrocuted. The nurses stood back for a second or two, then quickly got back to work. I sensed a lot of confusion in myself and the presence of the man next to me begin to dissipate. It all happened so fast that I couldn't quite recall much else after that, except for the fact that I never felt completely alone after that. I didn't have any time to long for anything more because I knew that there was never a time when this connection would be totally severed.

The next thing I remembered was waking up in my hospital bed knowing I had another day to live before I'd meet this man again. I didn't have the life experience to comprehend how amazing of an event I had just gone through, but this feeling of never being alone became quite prevalent in my life after that. It would take me a very long time before I realized how profound this experience was. Once I did, all the pieces of the puzzle were put together in a manner that would make all the pain of life understandably bearable.

Upon this realization, I was never really the same. I didn't have an inkling to let other people define my experiences and was able to see beyond what most people took for granted. As the years progressed, there was a deep sense of longing for that knowing again; to feel it closer to me, rather than just the comprehension of what I had gone through in the hospital that time. I didn't know who that man was, but I met him again almost twenty years later at just the perfect time to give me something to believe in again.

The concepts of feeling lost and found would plague me until I was almost forty years old; living in a world that felt so foreign to me, as if living in a dream until I would awaken again from a lifetime of slumber. I wanted so desperately to tell people about my experiences, but how do you articulate this type of knowing? So many people fear what they don't know and what they haven't consciously experienced themselves. This led to a lot of curiosity about life that had both positive and negative consequences.

Confessions of an Alleged Bottom

Genuine curiosity about sex didn't start at an early age. I wasn't molested as a child by a stranger in the park, nor did I ever grow excited upon seeing another boy naked in front of me in elementary school. In fact, I just wanted to be liked by one of them.

The interest slowly began when I noticed differences about myself that other people slapped a label on, hoping their intentional jeering would deter me from doing anything sinful or harmful. I played some sports but never considered myself an athlete by any means. I just wanted to make my parents proud of me even though I was usually left eating grass in right field. It was just something all boys were supposed to do and so I tried to do it, reluctantly.

My younger brother was the athletic genius of the family. It took everything in my power not to feel jealous of his lucky lot in life. He was quiet and handsome and was able to repel a lot the negative situations that I seemed to attract on a regular basis.

There was a soft nature to my appearance that many, including myself, didn't feel as being quite masculine enough. I expressed an interest in performing and before I knew it, I enrolled in a summer theatre camp playing an imp in a production of *The Snow Queen*, directed by Breezy Fenske.

She was a short, plump, loveable German lady whose fiery personality matched her burnt-sienna tanned, leathery skin. She wore bright makeup every day that accentuated her facial expressions but did little to draw attention away from her countless wrinkles.

Her white hair was cropped short and neatly bobbed just above the shoulders. When she turned her head, it would bounce and sway with each nod as she watched us improvise fairy tales for an hour and a half. I was very young and hardly knew what I was doing, but I had a wonderful time not having to know anything. From that point on, I knew that the performing arts would be a major part of my life.

After my stint as the green imp, I had a taste for the theatre. I thought it was cool that I was doing something other kids my age found odd, and most parents discouraged from their little boys' extra-curricular activities. Even then, it was apparent that I had an unfortunate penchant for non-conformity.

The following summer, I took a few art classes and enrolled in a basic vocal workshop with a rather eccentric voice teacher at a kid-friendly arts school called Arts Together. The sign on the door had little children holding hands with different color handprints around a picture of the Earth. I had a short but impressive solo in "The Lullaby of Broadway." My mother had to inch forward in her seat to hear my soft, soprano voice recount, "the daffodils who entertain at Angelo's and Maxies." I fought desperately to control my effervescent jazz hands and formidable Maxie Fords.

I had found my niche. I auditioned and was chosen to sing with the coveted Raleigh Boy Choir that fall and became an avid member of the St. Raphael's Catholic Church choirs. I took a tap-dancing class to test my natural prancing abilities and added a green sequined top hat to the green tights I wore as an imp the previous summer.

The boys and I ran around the room like chickens loosed from a pen. I waited patiently as my mother applied red lipstick and rouge to my cheeks with a disconcerted look on her face. I remember noticing how the mothers in the room had looks of disapproval on their faces, like somewhere down the line they may have screwed up parenting their little boys. Perhaps they breastfed too long, or simply not enough. Maybe taking Timmy to see the *Nutcracker* a few too many times was the straw that broke the camel's back.

Maybe her divorce from Larry, part-time mechanic, full-time anger-management drop-out, wasn't the best decision given the repercussions it had on their son's apparent lack of masculinity. I could almost hear their inner voices bemoaning, "I never should have bought him that tea set. What was I thinking?"

My mother knew very little about applying makeup. In all the years I'd known her she'd never had a manicure or let anyone touch her feet that didn't have a medical degree. Now she was responsible for dolling me up for Act II in the dance version of *The Wizard of Oz.* I was the only tap-dancing munchkin who looked like a two-dollar hooker that was hit by a Mack truck carrying a tank full of glitter and burgundy-tinted lip gloss.

Maybe an occasional sigh was all that was needed to convey her frustrations, but in her eyes there may have been far worse things I could have done with my time. These were the intimate conversation starters I longed for that my mother simply refused to have with her gay son.

I'd find rides, or my mother would drive me, to choir practice and piano lessons before the glorious day I received my driver's license. She'd attend my concerts and recitals when she could but would eventually fall asleep in the back of the auditorium. I'm sure that working the night shift for so many years was tough for any mother, but there were other options available that could have been better suited for a healthier family dynamic.

At this point, my life was consumed by the arts. I was constantly involved in the community having something or other to do with performing and volunteering. These activities became my safety net and trusted escape. There was so much room for growth and risk in an environment full of love and creativity.

Around the fifth grade, we moved from Raleigh, North Carolina to a town called Wayne, New Jersey. I went to three different schools in the fifth grade. We slept in a camper van for the summer, lived in a motel for a week, and then in the basement of my aunt's house before settling into a home with a babbling creek in the backyard.

I ended up attending Lafayette Elementary School, and although there wasn't a single Black student, there were enough Italians to fill a cannoli the size of a football field. It made me miss the South very much. It wasn't long before my brothers and I realized that moving to New Jersey was our family's last-ditch effort to find unity.

By then I had adjusted to life after cancer and was sad to have left the friends I had grown attached to while in Raleigh. I didn't like the aggressive way Northerners spoke. I missed good old-fashioned Southern hospitality, sweet tea, pulled pork, and social graces. I found New Jersey to be a bleak, dreadful place where trees clawed their way out from the Earth only to lie thin and naked for nine months out of the year. Cars were faster, louder, and so were the people.

There were a few times my younger brother would accompany my mother and I on our infrequent shopping excursions to discount clothing stores. On the way there, we would drive past the town's coveted nuclear power plant. We'd hold our breath until the building was out of sight because of the abominable testimonies my mother would recount about the physical effects of nuclear radiation exposure. We barely got all the way through the stoplight before one of us nearly passed out in the back seat. We thought if any of us took a breath near the facility that we'd be exposed to radiation and die. This was instilled in us by our mother who deterred us from playing in the rain for fear of being electrocuted by lightning. She also considered standing in front of the microwave a criminal offense and running with scissors to be punishable by death.

While all the other healthy boys were learning about sex and masturbation, I was much more interested in surviving the fifth grade without getting my face kicked in at recess. It took a lot of patience and introspection for me to accept the fact that I was different and that this quality didn't automatically make me a bad person. Still, being unable to vocalize my frustrations to anyone including my own mother built up a deep self-torment, which eventually turned into explosive anger during inopportune times.

"What are you doing, Danny?" I'd imagine mom asking.

"I'm playing billiards with Juan, my imaginary friend from Peru."

"Did you tell Juan to wipe his feet on the doormat before he came in from playing in the creek this afternoon? Who tracked in all this mud on the floor?"

My head spun around, and I began to projectile vomit through my eye sockets. With a look of disgust that arose from the Bogs of Eternal Stench, I retorted, "Juan does not hear you. Juan speaks Peru language and only knows three words: Hot chocolate, snow peas, and Ferrari. Juan does not like you for you reek of latex and baby powder!"

"Well, tell Juan, dinner's ready in five minutes. I'm making shake n' bake, macaroni and tuna, and watered-down ramen noodles."

As soon as she walked up the stairs into the steamy kitchen, I spun my head back around and began to wipe off the bile from my lower eyelids. Preparing myself to face my imaginary lover for one last time, I paused to ask Juan one final burning question.

I turned around and Juan was gone, leaving only a trail of mud through from the concrete basement to the wide-open patio screen door. Not only had mother scared off my Peruvian lover with her cooking, but in the absence to control myself, I had frightened away my one and only friend. That is until I was introduced to Frederick, a young, German American pilot who had an insatiable appetite for weekend antiquing. I acquired him up after reading *All Quiet on the Western Front,* while falling asleep during an all-*Antique Road Show* marathon.

I didn't understand it at the time, but our family dynamic was hanging on by a thin thread. My mother needed to be closer to her husband and her sons needed a stable father figure in their lives. She wanted us all to live together once and for all and this move was supposed to cure everything in one misguided but well-intended fell swoop. Sadly, that didn't happen as expected.

I didn't know how sad my mother was for so many years because she never let us know how she really felt. Call it a repressed Irish, Catholic thing, or simply a consequence of her similar upbringing. But my mother never sought help from anyone, nor did I ever see her in a stress-induced cleaning frenzy that would have triggered me to alert a medical professional. I was probably the closest thing she had to a confidant back then, and the only person who could empathically feel what she was going through. This made me feel obligated to her in a strange way and I took on more than my fair share of the emotional burdens for us both. She was stronger than an ox on the outside, but frail and broken in places where no one could see, as she continued to hide herself from the rest of the world.

We gave being together as a family a shot, but it would take years until my father would regain his composure as head of the household. This role was always being tested by my older brother who was a major fuckup. Until then, it was my mother who was responsible for maintaining a modicum of control and attempting to shield her younger children from the hardships of life by doing as little as possible. My father worked his tail off for us, but I didn't see him very often. So, to me he just wasn't around much. We ended up moving back to Raleigh that summer only this time with my father being a permanent fixture in our lives; for better or for worse.

Upon my father's return from business trips in previous years we used to shower him with welcome home parties. We'd make him banners and stand by the door with the porch light on so we could spot him pulling up into the driveway. He would bring us each a miniature toy from the airport, or if he was driving--which was usually the case--he would buy us a knick-knack from a convenience store off the side of the road. When we started getting older the parties stopped being fun and the free, plastic toys you'd get with the purchase of a McDonald's happy meal became less appealing as a token of his fatherly affection.

My father would pull me aside and say, "Now Danny, I've gotta go now. Look after Mommy and Erik…and make sure Mikey stays out of trouble. Can you do that for me, Danny boy?" I'd answer affirmatively because I knew how much he needed me to. He'd pat me on the head and tell me what a good boy I was. The pressures of life after cancer, of constant instability at home, of feeling so alone and taking care of everyone else's problems but my own were beginning to take their toll on me.

Moving back to Raleigh for middle school was a sigh of relief, but it was also where most of the problems in my social life emerged. Not only was I entering the sixth grade, but my soprano voice still hadn't changed and my chunky build that was acceptable in the North was now another chance for ridicule from the bullies at school.

The years of radiation and chemotherapy made my hair fall out and what grew back was fine and limp. I'd given up my outdated rat-tail for a perfectly groomed bowl cut parted straight down the middle of my head, which I would wash with Pantene Pro-V shampoo and conditioner every single day like clockwork. I would brush my hair back after parting it down the middle to allow the front hairs to dramatically fall to the sides exposing two well-maintained waves in the front. My hair eventually grew down to my mouth and I used it to cover myself when I needed to hide from others.

I'd pull the two magic front strands over my eyes and wiggle my nose a couple of times like *I Dream of Genie*, speeding me through any difficult situation unscathed. In doing so, my eyes wouldn't close until I knew I was safe and out of harm's way. This made walking in the hallways very difficult and getting lost an everyday occurrence.

I wore old hand-me-downs from my older brother, Mike, who had been stealing very expensive name brand clothing from local clothing stores and doing God knows what with his shitty friends. I watched my younger brother, Erik, get new clothes for school, as I stepped into the poor lighting of an insecure, confused middle child.

In middle school, I tried to remain as inconspicuous as possible hoping I wouldn't get stepped on by the bigger guys, but at the same time desperately looking for someone to find me and take me home as one of their pets. My older brother's reputation in the community was that of a thief: a no-good punk skateboarder and a disrespectful class clown who would rather do drugs than do his homework. So, I had the obligation of proving all the teachers wrong about our family. I realized later that it wasn't so much that I did it for them necessarily, but that I really enjoyed excelling at subjects that expanded my mind. I liked school and having structure in my life that was brimming with familial inconsistencies.

I created the most beautiful class projects and wrote the most imaginative school papers, but when it came time for gym class, I suddenly got an overwhelming urge to vomit up my corn flakes and powdered milk.

By the seventh grade, I got smart and started hanging out with the bad kids. They taught me how to sneak out of class, and I'd watch them smoke in the bathrooms without setting off the fire alarm. I felt more comfortable with outcasts knowing that deep down they felt the same way I did about practically everything. I wanted to be anywhere except the gymnasium, practicing my free throws or developing my one-armed cartwheels. When a fellow student smelled smoke coming from the girl's restroom, they alerted the teacher, and my friends and I were in navy-blue shorts and an oversized physical education t-shirt before we knew it.

I could hardly sit still waiting for my arts classes. As soon as the bell rang, I was out of my gym clothes and into my chair before the teacher had arrived. I used to have disturbing dreams of being chained to my desk in the old math trailer answering complex word problems while Ms. Hunter stood over me screaming into my ears and laughing with her booming voice reverberating off of the fake wooden panels on the walls. Turns out, I was just daydreaming in the back of her algebra class and waiting for life to pass me by. With drool oozing from my lower lip, I was called on to answer the next question.

"Umm...X=3," I'd whisper after a long and unnecessary deliberation.

"Wrong, Mr. Seda," she'd stab. "You're just like your brother."

The year flew by with the help of my best friend, Joel. He introduced me to all the bad things parents could ever hope their children to refrain from learning at such an impressionable age. I learned that those white stains on his blanket weren't toothpaste at all and that his love affair with *Beavis and Butthead* was contributing to his hyperactive behavior and lack of scholarly motivation.

His parents thought I was, sparing my effeminate ambiguity, a good role model. They might have been right, but every time one of our parents had to drive us to the mall, they would fume at our choice of music and our never-ending, laugh-out-loud fits at his latest joke or my spot-on imitations. I knew he wasn't a good influence on me, but somehow, I thought I could help him get through school and he would help me get through life for a while. I was almost waiting for something better to come along, but it never really did.

After a while I lost all my other friends. Joel and I's friendship became more of a drug addict clinging to their dealer for one last hit of laughter. In the end, I lost my best friend when our small group of degenerates crossed party lines. By the end of my eighth-grade year, I had lost all hope of gaining any self-esteem. All the energy I had left went into staying alive and keeping my head above water. It was the worst year of my life so far. Beating cancer was a synch, but crying myself to sleep every night and finding ways to end the torment alone was truly painful. I couldn't talk to anyone, let alone my mother, because she had enough problems.

That summer I went to the YMCA and worked out almost every day. I lost twenty pounds and began to get some muscular definition. The first day of high school everyone who knew me back in middle school could notice the improvements in my physical appearance and rising confidence level.

I tried out for the school play that fall. I didn't make the cut but the director, Mrs. Prater, pulled me aside and told me that she would be looking for me at the next audition. A couple of months went by and I worked up the courage to audition for the spring musical. I hadn't a clue what to sing and knew that singing anything from *Ace of Base* or Mariah Carey would get me in real hot water. I ended up choosing the "Star-Spangled Banner." We all had to line up on stage and once it was my turn I looked right into the lights like a diva and let loose. After I was done there was complete silence in the room.

In that moment, which to me felt like an eternity, I recalled the time in middle school when a frozen banana was thrown at me from across the cafeteria. Knowingly, I was expecting the same reaction with a head of cabbage or steaming pile of garbage. Those milliseconds were so frightening to me that I covered my head to block any sort of produce headed in my general direction from an audience of my peers.

Just then, everyone erupted in applause. I couldn't believe it! *Were they making fun of me or simply being patriotic? Could I have talent, or had I somehow ended up in a scene from Carrie?* I looked up to see if there was a bucket of blood being held over my head. It would take another year until I graced that stage for the first time. I was turned down that time by Mrs. Prater, but she told me to go talk to the music teacher and audition for the top choir. I followed her advice and finally found my sanctuary.

The choir director, Mrs. Marley, never let her hair down in public. She was the quintessential version of a Southern belle. She talked in her vocal break and often seemed frazzled. I made some great friends in choir over the next three years and had some of the best times of my life in high school.

A lot of life centered around after-school activities to prevent me from going home. To that end, I started running at night my junior year. It was a wonderful way to clear my head. I made it through pre-season for cross-country my senior year but quit before our first race, just in time to make it into the yearbook photos for doing something athletic. I was still too overweight and couldn't have handled the pressure of competing against seasoned runners at the time. I just didn't have the knack for sports that my younger brother did and so I continued pursuing the activities that I enjoyed and excelled in.

I didn't start dancing until college, but the moment I set foot on a real dance floor I never wanted to leave. I took my first ballet class my sophomore year and began pursuing life as a dancer from that point on. I was the kid who wanted to kick my legs and jump higher than anyone else in class and turn more than everybody, a regular Billy Elliott. I worked harder at it than anything I'd ever done, because it meant more to me than anything else I'd previously tried.

Running and dancing brought me great joy; an athletic and artful outlet that I could call my own. It gave me the opportunity to feel beautiful even when I didn't feel that way on either side. I could finally control something about my physical health, and it brought me so many wonderful experiences that I'd never dreamt were possible. I was hooked and desperately wanted more out of life.

It was at this time that I began to toying with the idea of moving to New York City after graduation. I was so heavily involved in the artistic community in Raleigh and at school that life seemed unsinkable for me back then. I started preparing to move and live the life of a performer, not knowing anything of what that would entail.

I met a young woman named Lindsay and had a two-year romantic relationship with her. I did my best to love her the way I had always wanted to be loved, and when our love affair ended, I was already in New York City, waiting to pick myself up off the ground again and live.

Scungili and Platanos in the Boogie-Down Bronx

New York wasn't the kind of place where you needed to go looking for trouble. Even if you didn't want any, it would find you, sooner rather than later. So, when my parents found out I was moving there after college they hoped it was just a phase; something I'd grow out of when I met the right girl. But my fear of dying a young, undiscovered talent ultimately took a backseat to my insatiable quest for knowledge and adventure. I moved to the big city with wide eyes, impossible expectations, and a whole lot of baggage.

The city was quite different from where I grew up. Within the southern comforts of middle-class suburbia, cow-tipping and late-night joyrides to the local Wal-Mart were the things to do when one was out of tobacco, cheap beer, or narcotics.

I was--for lack of a better description--a sensitive over-achiever, who began mastering the art of shapeshifting at an early age to make up for my abandonment issues and severe insecurities. I managed to give GI-Joe tea parties and random strip searches in complete secrecy, while concocting potions in the bathroom with watercolor paints and shampoo. I was convinced it made me invisible. Turns out I was just being ignored.

The six months I spent living in the Bronx at my grandparents' house was both a blessing and a curse. The best part was that I got to see my grandfather before he passed away, and the rest of my extended family whom I'd only seen during the Catholic holidays growing up: Christmas and Spring Break. What I wasn't expecting was an up-close and personal view into both of my parents' dysfunctional upbringing. It was there that I reached the conclusion that Hell did exist and was--in fact--nestled in a conjoined brick edifice on Bronxdale Avenue.

Living with grandma and working at the Pine Tavern was an incredible test of self-will. The lengths to which humans would go through to prevent themselves from living happy lives were of great interest to me. Being someone who learned from his mother that depression could be treated by a glass of white Zinfandel and a splash of gingerale, I was naturally opposed to believing anyone else had good reason to hate their lives. I was also under the impression that hiccups could be cured by chugging a cocktail of Aquafresh and tap water, until I got kicked out a friend's house for almost poisoning her son. Still, I was adamant to dive in headfirst, with my hands tied firmly behind my back and my mouth taped ever-so-loosely shut, as the semi-objective observer of a thing called "real life."

It was clear, at least to my grandmother, that life was a constant flagellation. Any happy thoughts were left to "dose beetches" walking up and down Bronxdale Avenue that she would mock from behind the uncomforts of her dimly lit living room and dingy windows barred horizontally by dusty, black blinds. Anyone caught smiling in her home was to be huffed at and made to suffer through a series of inaudible hexes and beratements in broken English with a heavy Puerto Rican sailor's tongue. Later, they were forced to rewash the dishes or re-arrange the empty, outdated condiment containers in her fridge according to the year of expiration. That way we'd remember just how awful life was supposed to be and how dreadful her life had most assuredly become.

My grandmother, Aida, was born in Cuamo, Puerto Rico. And that's really where the happy story ends. Her mother died when she was thirteen and after "acting up" she was sent to a local mental institution where she learned most of her odd adult behavior. She only left one light on in the whole house and had a strange obsession with picking things up and putting them back down again only after she'd already touched them once before; not to mention, recleaning everything anyone else touches in time to watch Telemundo and the daily horoscopes with Walter Mercado.

I was told stories of her heroic deeds at the institution when I was old enough to appreciate them. Apparently, she used to leave her bed at night and untie the screaming mental patients from their bindings. Something I'd never imagine her doing in a million years because it required a certain level of compassion that I wasn't entirely convinced she possessed.

It wasn't uncommon to see her standing in the dark at the kitchen sink; curlers gripping onto her dyed-orange hair, tied in black webbing atop her head, with a piece of ragged cloth holding the tight bundle together for dear life. Occasionally, a curler would come to its senses and try to make a run for it; silently and clumsily scaling down a clump of her thick, dry strands, only to end up on the floor, cowering beneath her massive stature and weight shifts like that of a drunken swagger. Hiding beneath the stove were six-legged creatures who loved to gobble up crumbs of crackers and stale bread that she'd haphazardly drop, as if watering a linoleum lawn.

Coffee was a must, and although I never understood the fascination adults had with their morning brew, it appeared to be one of the few joys my grandmother had in her life. She began her ritual with a deafening rumble of pots and pans that bellowed and clacked from within the cabinets above her broken and outdated oven. In twenty-five years, I'd never seen her use the damned oven. Yet, there it remained; a memento of crystalized time gone by. Never to return to its once pristine condition like that of her three children who by now had dysfunctional families of their very own.

The concept of a moment in history when grandma used to bake was upsettingly incomprehensible. I couldn't picture her calloused hands kneading dough, mixing up the ingredients for a secret family recipe of plantain-macadamia nut bread and placing it neatly onto an oven rack, or waiting patiently for her cupcakes to cool. Her Betty Crocker cookbook resting delicately on a bowl of fresh fruit, opened to page seventy-four: "How to bake brownies and other homemade sweet treats," with a spatula in one hand, a pink oven mitt in the other, and a smile that shined brighter than the tiles on her glistening kitchen countertops. "No way, Jose!" This image was ludicrous and would require too much evidence to validate later in therapy.

As soon as she selected the correct pot every living soul in the house could hear the sharp bangs of metal against the old wooden island that jutted out like a sore thumb dividing the dining room from the kitchen. I'd have the following imaginary conversation upon waking up to the ruckus down below me:

"Good morning, mi niñito! Did you sleep well?"

"Why yes, grandmother. Thank you!"

"I had no idea you woke up so early, young man. Can I get you some saltines and butter? Perhaps a nice Diet Pepsi to quench your morning thirst? There are exactly forty-five of them in the fridge lined up in five even rows of nine cans each."

"No thank you, grandma. I'm not that hungry. I'll just be in the shower dreaming of objects to shove into my arteries. On second thought, I'll be at the library all day today. I'm feeling extra inspired to write this morning."

The days weren't much different. I'd usually be gone running errands for grandpa, buying discount packages of bruised fruits, and refilling his daily prescriptions using his "Frequent Pill Poppers Advantage" card. If I had some time, I'd go into the city to take a dance class or purposely get lost on the 2-train since I didn't have to be at the restaurant until four in the afternoon. Anything that kept me moving and out of the house. I learned that technique from my father.

I told grandma where I was going and gave her a goodbye kiss on her saggy, rubbery cheeks before I left. Her response was always the same. "Ho-Keh, Meesta Beeg Chot! Joo gonna leef downtown now, ehh? Hwell, mehbee joo chould tink abou leefin dare instead off een MI CASA! Oh-Keh…eh, ehh?"

If by some stroke of bad luck, I was left with nothing to do all day but watch Fox News and hear grandma sigh for the eighty-eighth time, "Aye, Yeesus Chriis," I'd make believe I had another job in the city that required my immediate attention. I would tell her not to wait up, as I was sure that this could be the one gig that would undoubtedly make me rich and famous. She would huff and mumble something in jaded old lady under her breath in a shadow of the hallway as she unwillingly opened each dead bolt on her lead-lined front door. I'd round the corner of her brownstone heading to work at the restaurant after closing the rusted metal gate behind me, feeling the chill of her stare until I was clean out of sight. Then, like clockwork, she would dead-bolt herself into her three-floor confinement, peek through one of the black, dusty blinds, and renew her daily snoop fest.

One evening at the restaurant, I was up to my ears in drama. "A few more hours of this and I'm walking out of this joint," I coolly remarked to anyone within earshot. As I rounded the hostess stand to begin my duties, Jerry, the manager, asked me for a plastic cup of water to mix a discrete concoction of protein powders. This was as vital for inclusion as an inner-city Italian man as were eyebrow waxings, manicures, and a valid tanning salon membership.

Jerry enjoyed telling other people what to do but watching them scurry across the floor like rats without proper instruction was an even bigger thrill. It was part of his character and fine, Mafioso-style, purebred Italian upbringing. Besides the fact that he got a haircut every week and skimmed a little off the top of our earnings each night, he was quite an enjoyable fellow to have on your side in a disagreement.

I returned, cup in hand, and reluctantly gave it to him like a nurse giving his patient a quick fix. Like a good junkie, Jerry carefully mixed his ingredients to the correct consistency and guzzled it down in one manly gulp. "Atta boy," I mumbled through gritted teeth, never fully understanding why people need to lose precious neck space to feel more in control of their lives.

After he left for the gym, customers began cautiously trickling into the restaurant like there was a discount bake sale at a school for the blind. I was ready to start making money and prayed that nothing would go horribly wrong that evening. I noticed each waiter popping in and out of the breakroom with pasta lodged between their lips and a scowl on their face, staring down the clientele that they would reluctantly have to wait on. I began to take tables like I always did with a grin and a hurried chassé. The night was long and grueling but the extra eighty dollars in my pocket was cause for celebration.

Before leaving, I picked up my coat off the breakroom floor and noticed it had been rummaged through. I found a note in my right front pocket that read, "Call me After work if you wanna *Play* at my Place." I knew exactly who wrote it. It reminded me of those mysterious notes left by serial killers who used ripped letters from magazines to mask their identity. By analyzing the syntax and pre-pubescent handwriting it was clear that I wanted nothing to do with this person. So, I stuffed the note in the back pocket of my jeans along with my pride.

I took the note home and threw it on my computer, so I'd remember to use it for writing inspiration in the morning. I was still fighting a cold and the stress of work was getting to me. I couldn't sleep and I'd wake up every morning at the crack of dawn just to hear the morning commuters on their way to work. If I was smart, I would have quit the day before to leave all the crap for some other unlucky stud with dreams of making quick, easy money. Somehow the fascination with learning and making my own living deterred my decision-making process for the time being. I slowly transformed into another working-class stiff caught in a false perception of: "That's just the way life is supposed to be."

As the third month steamrolled by, my grandmother and I had established an uneasy truce with one another. I didn't touch her shit unless I desperately needed to and would always put it back at precisely the angle at which it was found. Then, she didn't loathe the sight of me as much as she did when I first arrived.

I think what buttered her up were the cheeseburger deluxes I'd come home with every now and then from her favorite diner. One time she even shouted, "Ooh-la-lah!" when she opened the to-go container and found that the French-fries were still hot and crispy. You see, over the years my grandfather brought back food from his daily trips around the neighborhood. It took him a good hour to get in and out of transportation, so I imagine the food was devoid of any warmth until zapped in a microwave for two minutes on high. Grandma was still afraid to use the damn thing since an earlier episode at my aunt's house when she left a Lean-Cuisine in too long and almost burnt down their Pompton Lakes estate.

Once in a blue moon, I'd see her in something other than a weathered, floral-print housedress and beat-up sandals with flaking gold paint and plastic jewels super-glued on top of thin, lingering straps. Except for monthly doctor's appointments or immediate family emergencies, she'd only venture out into the sunlight when necessary. She had no problem snapping a cockroach in half with her thumb and index finger, but taking a walk outside in the fresh, urban air was frightening; hence, it was completely out of the question.

While most people enjoy sleeping under the covers, my grandmother insisted on going to bed on top of her comforter with a different blanket pulled high above the head. Her room was totally off limits to everyone. It wasn't a written rule, but it was just something we never did growing up and were never told not to as far as I can remember. I guess the overwhelming smell of musk and impending sense of doom got the best of us, and there were simply other rooms to fear and other plastic couches to sit on that made grandma's room just one more place we weren't supposed to touch or enjoy.

That night, awoken by a piercing urge to urinate, I walked down the hallway to the bathroom passing her bedroom. Everything inside of me wanted to keep going toward the only moonlight I could see trying its damnest to shine through the opaque window above the shower. My curiosity got the best of me, and I stopped at the doorframe for a long, hard look.

In the darkness, I saw the silhouette of what appeared to be a mummy. Its hands were neatly crossed, and its legs were squeezed together in an almost ritualistic fashion. I wondered; *what kind of person sleeps in such a deliberate position?* Was she afraid of dying in her sleep, or hoping to do so and afraid that no one would find her before the rigor mortis set in? Instead of troubling the coroner with unruly stiff limbs, she learned to sleep like a budding butterfly securely fastened in her cocoon. The whole scene was beautifully tragic to behold, but morbidly romantic and peculiarly disturbing to have to witness.

The next morning I woke up to the sound of my alarm singing a fast-paced mazurka I hadn't memorized fully in one of my many music history classes. The melody was completely out of place for my current dwelling and made me question where I was at the time. So after shaking my head and rubbing my eyes I changed it to Chopin's *Funeral March.* That way I'd wake up each morning without any false expectations of finding happiness, ready to wage chemical warfare with the infestation of cockroaches that frequented our humble abode.

An Afternoon Gaydream

It's amazing the things that come to mind while you're ironing your underwear. I recall the time I worked on Fire Island one sweltering summer weekend when I was twenty. I needed some extra cash and a manager at a dance studio I worked at gave me the job, saying it would be "an eye-opening experience." Intrigued, I gave it a shot. At this point, I was still playing it straight and approaching my senior year in college. I had to take the train, a cab, and a ferryboat just to get to work. I thought of it as an adventure and a great way to get out of the Bronx for a while.

To anyone who doesn't know what Fire Island or Cherry Grove is, you've probably never been to the ballet or had your chest waxed. It's the gay Mecca of paradise islands. I had no idea what to expect, which was probably a good thing now that I think about it.

At the time, I really wanted to have the fact that I could very well be gay stomped into pieces especially now that I was graduating from college. I was "supposed" to get married, have two children, and write dreamy literature in the attic office of my duplex in Raleigh. Much like I had done before, I looked for every chance I got to prove myself wrong for the things I instinctively knew were true. I hoped this experience would change my mind and end up "scaring me straight."

I stepped off the boat to find men in rainbow Speedos, shouting at one another with pom-poms and beaded necklaces hanging from their once-taut chests. Now saggy and tanned, bald, and droopy, these men looked more like circus clowns doused with kerosene and set on fire, instead of travelers seeking respite from life in the big city.

I was alone, very young, and in-shape; not a good combination on a faux-tropical island full of hungry bears. I felt so out of place because I was still calling myself straight or bi or the opposite of whatever I was denying at the time. Meanwhile I'd have this mental conversation with myself: *I was not raised like this. Well, I wasn't really raised at all. I'm supposed to be the good son, right? Ooh, is that Alec Baldwin?*

I kept a low gaze as I proceeded down the boardwalk to the Belvedere Hotel. The Belvedere was a landmark. The gates were impressive--about thirty years ago--and now creaked as I entered. There was a black and white cat that welcomed me with a hiss. I dodged an unraveled water hose and walked past the outdoor showers making my way to the front desk to meet my new colleagues.

My first assignment was to clean and turn down all the rooms. I was to assist a man named Giulio. At least that's what the sticker nametag read on his rear-end. All the rooms had a specific theme: the Grecian, the Roman, the French and the Dungeon Rooms all proudly displayed the essence and history of fornication throughout the centuries. The walls were painted with peculiar little accents that made you crick your neck in disbelief. It was like watching Carol Channing win an arm-wrestling contest. You want to enjoy it, but you just don't get it, nor do you know how to stop looking at it in disbelief.

My room was next to Giulio's in the old pool house that had recently been converted into something resembling the servant's quarters from a porn shoot. Come to think of it, I don't remember seeing any other employees where Giulio and I had to stay. We were partitioned off from the rest of the hotel and forced to share a makeshift pool-house that reminded me of a tiny boat cabin with a rustic, trailer-park motif. I guess it was par for the course since we were the lowest on the totem pole that summer, and I doubted wanting to stay there any longer than those next two days.

At dinner, I was introduced to the Dom of the establishment. He looked older than Jesus and surprisingly had all his teeth between his sunken, overused lips. His eyes and quiet demeanor told me more about his long, adulterated history than any of the stories his admirers regaled us with as we passed the soup bowl around the grandiose dining room table. The entire event was something out of the 1991 movie *Nothing but Trouble.*

I was frightened and intrigued all at the same time. I didn't know what I was doing, but it was totally out of my comfort zone and I thoroughly enjoyed that. Thankfully, I had no serious urges to do anything other than work that weekend and enjoy the spectacles that were all around me. I knew where it would have led me if I got sucked into the evil clutches of temptation: a trip to the health clinic, an apartment in Chelsea, and a studded dog collar with my name on it.

The next day, I was called in to fix one of the outdoor showers by the veranda. The fake palm trees were standing motionless in the hot, hazy air that accentuated the faux Florida vibe. A non-working fountain was in the center of the patio, and lounge chairs were strewn about the concrete floor, as if a family of Grizzly bears had rummaged around a campsite looking for meat. I was working on the damn thing for a good half an hour, trying to act like I knew what water pressure was, when a handful of men started rearranging the broken lounge chairs to get a better view.

Apparently, my friend Ken was playing a trick on me that I wasn't aware of. He had alerted the other visitors of the hotel that there was a "straight" guy trying to fix a shower by the veranda at noon that day. I had no idea until he came out and told me to stop embarrassing myself. Even then it took me a while to understand what he was talking about.

"You're so gullible, Dan." I punched Ken on the arm in my best heterosexual display of fraternal comradery.

Ken took me to a party off the property that evening to make up for his shenanigans. I was greeted with open arms by two gigantic drag queens who kissed me on both cheeks, leaving lipstick and globs of sweaty make-up on my face. Everyone was grinning from ear to ear and raising their hands up in the air yelling happily at each other to make their love handles less obvious. They were having some sort of a pool contest and I cringed, clinging on to Ken as my life-preserver. He rolled his eyes, accepting his responsibilities, and took me around to meet the rest of his friends.

Everyone knew and respected him on the island. We ate on the beach, drank a beer in public, which was new to me at the time and later he took me to a mutual friend's house as a surprise. I rang the doorbell and it chimed, "I will survive" by Aretha Franklin. Tim, our ex-coworker from the dance studio answered the door in a Hawaiian skirt and coconuts on his chest strung together by neon-orange shoelaces. I hadn't laughed that hard in a while. Tim had recently come out and bought a nice place right on the island with the money he made from publishing his novel. He welcomed us all into his home and introduced us to his partner.

After seeing his perfect home, meeting his perfect partner and their perfect, adopted Schnauzer, I snooped around to find any evidence of foul play. I noticed pictures of them on trips to far off lands, by the side of a small airplane, and underneath a waterfall holding hands. On Tim's computer, the screensaver was a picture of the happy couple smooching with smiles on their faces. I sat back in his office chair and heard the men laughing and chatting downstairs wondering where I was.

I began to realize that it wasn't a mystery any longer. It wasn't a question of lifestyles or preferences but simply a matter of living and loving. There were big gays and small gays, old gays and new gays, normal gays and off-the-charts, crazy gays. Once I began to open my eyes to see other people without having to label them, I didn't see what was so odd about the whole thing anymore. Why people can be so hurtful about others enjoying and living life was beyond me. I began to feel sad that I looked down on the very people whom I was beginning to see that I had the most in common with.

The Repercussions of Playing It Straight

It wasn't until I was in college that I even toyed with the idea that I might be gay. I had had an indescribable relationship with a man named Matthew when I was nineteen that lasted three years and ended abruptly. I was in love with him but couldn't admit it to myself, so I fought it with everything I had. He joined the Air Force to "straighten up" and I was left in great despair with a broken heart. He only really kissed me once. No one could know about our dirty little secret, although from the looks of things everyone knew…except us.

From that point on, my life took a major turn and could only be characterized as a fight for happiness. Senior year of college I met Lindsay in rehearsals for *Cabaret*. I was the lead, and she was a chorus girl. We instantly fell for each other, and she changed my world that had been ravaged by heartache, confusion, and guilt for years. She brought color and joy into my life, the likes of which I'd never seen from anyone else. The first year was magic and we soon decided to move in together into our very first New York City apartment after I graduated from NC State.

She was a virgin in every sense of the word. Although my love affairs had been few, they were passionate and enveloping, and I did know what it was like to be intimate with both sexes. I welcomed her innocence and her soft, pale skin. We lived in an incredible apartment on the Upper East Side on Lexington Avenue, and played house very well. We had jobs that were feet away from our apartment and blocks from the private college she transferred to. Life looked perfect.

One evening, I came home from a hard day of auditions and working late at the restaurant to find our apartment devoid of life. I was dumbfounded. The door slammed shut and I dropped the keys in the bowl beside our tiny kitchen table as I had done a hundred times before. I propped my back against the door and slid down the cold metal surface for what seemed like an eternity. It was bound to happen, and perhaps the whole thing was long overdue.

Lindsay hadn't been eating normally for the past several months. Instead of counting calories, she began to measure all her food into tiny quantities, and eventually stopped eating my cooking altogether. Our sex life dwindled to once a week, then to once a month, and then to nothing at all. We acted like roommates, and I had the creeping suspicion that this "little gay thing" I could never quite manage to get off my chest was beginning to take over. It was getting too complicated living a mental double life, so after she left for good, I writhed on the floor for three days then fucked the first guy I could.

I was alone in the apartment with the sounds of traffic on Lexington Avenue screeching outside the window. All I wanted to do was jump off the fire-escape. The reality I had tried so desperately to create had crumbled in front of my eyes. After years of pretending to be someone else, I had no idea how to pick up the pieces of my current situation. There was no one I could call that would understand what was really going on, mainly because I couldn't face the truth inside myself. I took my keys and left Manhattan, driving back home to North Carolina to do some serious soul-searching.

I didn't want to be gay. I didn't want my life to be consumed with the meaningless sex that is so often portrayed. I hadn't seen any healthy gay relationships and everything I was told about gay people growing up scared the hell out of me. I wanted to know that I could honestly love a man and have that love returned openly and honestly before I would ever even utter the words to myself.

I stayed with my parents for a few months and began to unravel the mysteries of my existence. I met my first gay couple and saw with my own eyes the love that these two men shared together. I observed them from every angle, and even lived with them for a week to make sure their relationship wasn't just a figment of my imagination. I steadied myself in a new belief that indeed love between two men did and can exist in a normal, productive way. It turned everything I knew about the world on its head.

Kevin and Greg were two men I had met through a mutual acquaintance in the theatre community. Greg was a prominent figure in the non-profit sector and made his living helping and teaching people to live healthy, active lives. Kevin worked for the government and held a quiet stable job downtown. They had two dogs named T.J. and Max whom they loved dearly and treated as their own children. They had a townhouse, and it was always kept neat and clean. Greg wouldn't have it any other way.

I eventually moved back to New York City with an entirely different outlook on life. I was still a little wary about stepping completely out of the closet, so I chose to focus on my performing career and dive headfirst into the wild and exciting world of auditions, networking, and unemployment. It was there that I met the man I would consider to be the first guy I ever openly dated.

I was fascinated by the idea that I could hold his hand in public and rub noses with him while sitting on public park benches. It was the first time I could let my guard down and be myself. We shared a little bit of our hearts and I was content for a time. I didn't want anything more at that point. I just wasn't ready. He fell in love with me, as was the case in many of my previous relationships with women, but I ran from it like I always seemed to do so well.

I realized that indeed I was gay and there was no longer any reason to hide from it. That night I made the permanent change to the sexual orientation information on my Myspace page. It seemed like such a small and inconsequential move, but for me it was unequivocally the boldest thing I'd ever done. I wasn't afraid of inevitable rejection.

By this time, it was October of 2006 and I was living in Harlem with my friend Carmen. I met her at an audition in the Actors' Equity building and after sharing a slice of pizza and a Dr. Pepper she made me a copy of the keys to her apartment that her gay granduncle bought in the 1930s. He'd only visit maybe twice a year and his room was kept exactly as it had been since the end of the Second World War. He had survived being gay and Black in Harlem and had witnessed the birth of the Harlem Renaissance.

That November, I attended a meeting at the local LGBT center and met a man named Andrew. He was a vice president at NBC and headed up the local chapter of the Human Rights Campaign in New York City. Through him I met Mel, who was the head of Soulforce, a national organization dedicated to ending religious and political-based oppression against LGBT people. The timing was perfect! I didn't even know what LGBT was at the time, but after hearing Mel speak at a Unity Church service that Sunday, I decided to see what all the fuss was about. From there I met Haven, who was a co-director of something called the Equality Ride. I quickly went on tour with the campaign, challenging colleges and institutions of higher learning that had discriminatory policies against lesbian, gay, bisexual, and transgender individuals. That March I joined Soulforce and headed out West with the Equality Ride 2007.

I studied the Bible front to back and read other religious texts and spiritually inspirational books for LGBT youth. My time in Harlem ended that December and I went home to Raleigh to produce a benefit concert for Soulforce and the upcoming Equality Ride. I planned the concert from the ground up and spent every waking moment for the next two months working to ensure it was a success. We ended up breaking even, but the toll it took on me personally was immense.

Directly after the concert I hopped on a plane to join our fellow riders in Minneapolis. There we learned how to peacefully demonstrate our views to those who would be screaming obscenities at our faces. We were taught how to fall to the ground in a ball to protect our vital organs from kicks and punches. We were inspired by the work of Dr. Martin Luther King, Jr. and Mahatma Gandhi. Their philosophies on life, peace, and stillness in the most desperate of times were inspiring to me in impactful ways.

We got onto our respective buses and parted ways. I would never see my friends from the East bus again. Two weeks before our scheduled homecoming, I would have to leave due to health reasons. I had suffered a mental breakdown, so I got on a plane back to Raleigh feeling defeated and shaky in the hopes of seeking answers and help.

My entire immediate family met me at the airport. This had never happened before. The whole family being in one place at the same time without fighting was unfathomable to me. I couldn't look at any of them for long. I never asked them to come, and it was clear that my mother had told everyone what happened even though I had asked her not to. All I wanted was to be dropped off at a mental institution for evaluation.

My older brother, Mike, held packets of printouts in his hand that he scavenged for online about the possible mental disorders he subsumed I had. It was his manipulative way of helping the situation. Erik had no idea what to do for me, so he just stood there quiet as usual. His reaction didn't surprise me; he had never seen me in such a state. I was usually so together for him. After all, I was usually the one helping him learn life's important lessons. My father was silent. My mother had been crying and was afraid to touch me. It all felt like relatively normal reactions in its dysfunctionality and was yet another indication that I was not going to get what I needed from any of them.

I warded off their superficial platitudes like a movie star rebuffing the opportunistic paparazzi and asked my mother to drive me to the hospital. My family pleaded with me to come home and assured me that if I did, "All will be better in the morning." Tired of dragging myself through explanations of what I needed that they could never understand, I fought for my own wellbeing and told my mother to drive me to Holly Hill. Unfortunately, they couldn't understand that they were in no position to help me because they never helped or tried to before. There were a lot of unexpressed issues that I just could not articulate at the time, especially since the family would not accept them or appreciate their magnitude.

I arrived at the hospital past midnight. A kind woman at the desk looked at me and immediately called the intake counselor. Her name was Hope and she treated me with more nurturing kindness than I was led to believe I deserved. She asked me the tough questions and I responded with honesty. She said that I wasn't crazy and that I didn't belong in the hospital, but that outpatient care was available if I wanted it.

I fought with her to stay the night because I just couldn't go home to people who would have continued to trivialize the matter or find convenient ways to deflect a collaborative sense of responsibility. Hope looked directly at me and lovingly said, "Please go home. I'll see you in the morning. I promise. Here's my card. Call me if you need anything in the meantime." With that I was out the door in a matter of minutes. My mother was seated in the warmth of her SUV with the headlights on looking eerily repugnant in the moonlit mist. She was so good at playing the victim when others needed support. Her demeanor only added to my embarrassment and despondency.

I reluctantly got into the car and she drove me back to the house in complete silence. I could feel her anger and disgust at my decision to seek viable help. Nothing about my mother was ever compassionate or warm. When we got home, I quickly went upstairs to my bedroom. I slept longer than I'd ever slept in my life.

I was the first to arrive at the hospital for outpatient care the next day. There, I began what I like to consider "Brain School." This included group and individual counseling, dialectic behavioral therapy, role play and dyadic training, with lunch in the hospital cafeteria. I saw my first real therapist, a psychiatrist named Dr. Squarer. He gave me a handful of Ambien, a prescription for 20 milligrams of Prozac, and labeled me with the diagnosis of recurrent moderate to major depression. I graduated from the program in five days since my insurance wouldn't cover a full week.

I made a vow to myself, and much like any other promise, I always do my best to keep it. I took over all my financial responsibilities from my parents. They would no longer use this to control me. I got three jobs that summer and earned my yoga teaching certification from Asheville Yoga Center that July. My time spent there in the mountains of Western North Carolina was exactly what I needed to engender the healing process. There, I met amazing people who will forever be remembered as changing my life.

After coming back from Asheville, I sold everything I owned. I wanted to start over. I had yard sales, garage sales, sold a few items on online auctions, and made donations to Goodwill. After giving back my last item, the car I'd had since I was a senior in high school, I took the last few bags and bought a one-way ticket to Penn Station.

On the train ride there, I sat next to a woman and a priest. It turns out that she was a very prominent figure in American history (she was the first female postmaster general) and that the priest was a world traveler and an admittedly jovial alcoholic. We recounted tales of our lives all the way to New York City. Once I arrived at the end of the line, Carmen was there waiting for me.

I started over again. I reclaimed my right to personal happiness. I struggled hard. I lost some battles but won others. I landed a few good jobs and lost others. I settled into a steady rhythm that was finally leading to independence, even though it was far from easy.

For the first time in a while, I recalled a conversation that my chosen mom, Judy, and I had in her kitchen in Raleigh one afternoon. This must have been when I was in my early twenties since I had looked to her for the kind of motherly attention and support that I desperately needed since I was 19 years old. She was pivotal in helping me get through several periods of my life that would have otherwise left me for dead.

Judy was a very intuitive foster mother of three, who had prophesized that I'd move back to the big city and meet a man there that would end up changing the course of my life. She had always been right before, so there was no reason to think otherwise this time. Her prediction was the only thing I had left to believe in, so I gave it everything I had. It was my last-ditch effort to find happiness even if it hadn't happened yet. I gave up everything I had to find myself in the process.

Conversations with a Waiter

I tended to attract friends who lived vicariously through all my crazy Goonie adventures. This usually left them craving for more unbelievable stories, which I'd eventually divulge under increasing peer pressure. The longer I entertained them with every huge, embarrassing failure, the more I'd question where the stage I seemed to reside upon began and ended. I'd leave them all grinning from ear to ear, but obviously feeling thankful that they didn't have to be me.

When you're down and out it is usually because you put yourself there. Either you don't believe you deserve any better, or you just give up thinking there are other alternatives to misery. It's a quixotic notion that is both overrated and severely misunderstood by people who have normal lives and stable jobs. I used to believe in the old cliché that to be a successful performer you must be a starving artist first. At least that's what all the movies portraying downtrodden heroes--played by such stars as Leonardo DiCaprio and Mel Gibson--led me to believe. That would be fine if you looked at life as a long string of successive tests provided to prove yourself worthy to some guy on a cloud who is holding your dreams just a few inches out of reach. I grew to consider myself a worldly connoisseur of imbroglio: it just so happened that I chose a profession that rewarded that kind of personal torment.

For two full days of dishonest work, I worked at a place called Miracle Spa near Penn Station. The madam, Jimmy, kicked me out in a manic episode when he found out I was being too honest with clients. I was an illegal masseur giving a few grown men hand jobs for a hundred dollars a pop. There wasn't much room for denial, in my opinion. After that foray into hard labor, I chose to hand out flyers in Times Square for ten dollars an hour as something called a "promotional model" or "brand ambassador," depending on which corporate entity you were beholden to at the time. This basically meant that I was performing a similar job to an illegal masseur--only this time I was legal, paid taxes, and handed out advertisements for diet supplements instead of handjobs.

Then, I waited tables in a handful of restaurants; so much so, that my resume began to grow as long as a CVS receipt. That seemed to be the only saving grace throughout my disastrous life as a "starving artist." It was the only "real" job I could consistently fall back on when things got bad. The best part about being a waiter was that I got to eat, which was literally a matter of life and death back then. Even if we weren't supposed to eat at work, I made sure to snack, and took the rest home in a tinfoil swan. I ate bread, olives, and soda water for an entire summer. Not because I was dieting, but because it was the only thing I could get away with eating while literally working my ass off. I lived off bread and butter at a French bistro near the East River. They had little bottles of soda that I'd take on special occasions to lift my drowning spirits.

I learned so much about life being a waiter. I learned how to handle money quickly and responsibly and how to deal with difficult people through conversation and food. The one thing that was consistent for me then were the other waiters. They were always looking for something else to do other than what they were doing at the time. So, naturally, I fit right in. I used to think that waiters were all just lost alcoholics looking for a rest stop in purgatory. It was a transitory lifestyle that appealed to me then because I wasn't the only one with my fingers crossed for something better half the time.

Everyone was hoping for their big break, a starring role on *Days of our Lives,* or the chance to meet a big record producer at their next table. Dancing servers gracefully chasséd into and out of the kitchen balancing trays of sashimi and sake on their heads, while singing waiters resented the fact that their solo career was being put on hold to wish a spoiled brat at table 12 a happy birthday.

Nothing was stable, not even the menus. But there was a soft humming sound that kept everything operating together in a manageable flow. One could have assumed it was the refrigerators, that if broken would have ruined everyone's evening. Instead, there was an inexplicable rhythm that emanated with every clink of glassware and clank of metal pans. The cacophony made me feel less like a servant and more like an entrepreneur of my own mini real-estate enterprise. At the end of the night, I'd go back to my tiny apartment, crawl into bed, and then get up and wash my sheets in the bathtub because they reeked of halibut and soup du jour.

When it wasn't busy, I polished glassware as a meditative practice. Staring out of the windows, I'd dream of where exactly I went wrong. Sometimes, I would bring my notebook with me and stash it behind the receipt printer. I'd scribble at the bar until an angry man in a tweed suit demanded a Glenfiddich on the rocks without the slightest hint of eye contact or personal recognition. I'd pour his poison and watch him pile drive his ringed paws into the thinly sliced, waffle potato chips that were lightly sprinkled with sea salt and freshly ground pepper, delicately and proudly displayed on a paper doily in an artfully decorated porcelain bowl.

One regular used to sit at the corner of the bar and order a white wine spritzer with a twist of lime. She would tell me stories of her travels rivaling those of Jonathan Swift and Mark Twain in imagery and succulence. With the nozzle in my hand, I'd pour carbonated water into a squeaky-clean glass filled half-way with a California chardonnay, listening to Madame Tussaud describe her days riding on the backs of African elephants. With her serving staff of "twenty, some odd" and her father the explorer/philanthropist leading the pack, young Tussaud was fed her meals by hand and showered with riches her entire life. When her husband died, she had nothing to do all day but find twenty-somethings willing to humor an old lady with an open ear. We gathered around the bar, mesmerized by her heatstroked adventures, seeing the distant tundra through her sparkling eyes.

The restaurant was called Willow. Before we broke up, my girlfriend and I named our kitten after the place, since it was across the street from where we lived on Lexington Avenue. There was an amazing view from the second floor where I could see the window to our apartment building directly over Swifty's. I used to watch the bus scoot down the street and jealously grimace at all the predictable, upper-class people going about their lives.

It was always a spectacle to see what they were wearing and how trapped they seemed to look walking down the street in shoulder-padded blazers and cuffed slacks; how their colicky children behaved toward their immigrant nannies who were too afraid to discipline them for fear of deportation. I wished a lot back then for just a glimmer of what they had because it seemed like the world was their oyster and catered to their every whim.

Once an older couple was seated outside the restaurant and engaged me for a brief time in conversation while I rested plates of dirty dishware between my wrist, thumb, and pinky. They spoke about how lucky I was to have my whole life ahead of me, and how they would trade everything to have the health that I possessed.

I looked at them and said, "I'd give anything to have half of what you walk home with every day."

The man looked at me and took out a pen and paper. He wrote down the numerical version of "$1.00."

He said, "See. Look there. What's that?" I told him that it was a dollar.

He added, "What would it look like if I added another zero?"

Thinking I was being quizzed on my math skills, I said hesitantly, "That would be ten dollars, Sir. You just have to move the decimal place."

"Yes. That's right. And so on and so forth. You see there, son. It's just a dollar with a couple of extra zeros added on to it. If you think about it all in dollars and cents you see it's all just a game."

I looked at him and half understood what he was talking about. I went back to my daily routine and went home to do the same thing the following day.

The next evening I was polishing silverware and placing it in the correct position on the clothed napkins for lunch service. I looked out the window to see what I could find to take my mind off what I was doing.

Poodles with tufts of curly hairs protruding from their backsides gleefully paraded by. Chihuahuas looking like overgrown rats with spikey haircuts were stuffed in pink purses that dangled from women's wrists like charm bracelets. I began to write a few paragraphs in my head when my daydream was interrupted by the manager who needed me to haul up a box of wine from the cellar. "Back to the rat race," I told myself, breaking out of bliss.

The Bangladeshi busboys were always fighting by the downstairs broom closet about American politics and the differences between various ethnic groups. When I entered the hallway leading down to the cellar, they headed straight for me. With flat palms facing my direction, they shrugged shoulders and bobbed their heads yapping about this president and that president wondering what I thought about Muslims. I tried not to get involved, so I asked them if they knew if staff dinner was ready.

Diana Krall massaged my ears through the sound system as I dodged the mildewed pipes in the basement, kicking over rattraps and brushing away sticky paper like an explorer in some lush undiscovered jungle. Heaving up the metal staircase, I began to hear Diana through a garbled haze of detectible plosives knowing I was almost out of the dungeon into my next level of Hell. Entering through the heavy plum-colored curtains that separated the kitchen from the downstairs dining room, the smell of fresh city rain seemed to drown out my pain for a while. I made Alana, the manager, smile with my storied antics about the Bangladeshis, which had two effects: it made her like me long enough to keep me from doing more physical labor, and exposed her rotten teeth which made us both feel apologetically uncomfortable.

I had a natural knack for making people laugh, usually at the expense of my own pride. In whatever type of people I was around, I always seemed to win at games like "Have You Ever." No matter the question, I usually experienced the event on one level or another. This ability would keep the crowd entertained for hours leaving me time to plan my exit strategy. Who else could say, that they were deported from Jamaica for being incorrectly profiled as a suburban drug dealer, or was seriously considered for the role of "fart technician" in a NY Fringe Festival musical flop?

What other idiot would wear black dress socks and sneakers to a corporate job interview, teach naked water aerobics at a nudist resort, and race a crazed lunatic down I-95 for two and a half terrorizing hours? How could someone answer a Craigslist ad to transport a desk from North Carolina to New York in 24 hours, get hit by a taxi on 33rd and Park Avenue, and be denied from voluntarily admitting themselves into a mental institution?

My friends would all agree that no matter where they were in life or what horrible situations they found themselves in, they could always cheer themselves up by listening to another one of Dan's crazy adventures. I suppose this was why my name was perpetually stamped on the guest list at parties, and why I constantly found myself stopped and frisked at random screenings in airports.

A Weekend to Remember

I looked in the mirror and recoiled at the glowing red sight that lay before me. The look on my face at my own reflection could have frightened small children at play. Sheer panic and confusion graced an almost splotchy, ruby complexion, and my eyelids refused to open all the way. I looked more like a hungry twelve-year-old Cambodian boy who fell asleep on top of a rock during the summer solstice than a guy who had just come back from an afternoon day trip to Wrightsville Beach.

Not fully understanding why God curses those of Northern European ancestry with such a painful reminder of their heritage, I proceeded to disrobe for my morning shower and glanced down toward my swollen feet. In the mirror was a toasted gringo who had red patches of burnt, peeling skin around his cheeks and under his eyes, a tan line as thick as stripes on the American flag, and a bare ass so white it could safely guide ships home in the dark.

Athena, who was a dear friend of mine from high school, and I had no idea that our dinner date would end up lasting the entire weekend. Spaghetti, salad, and a bottle of merlot was just an appetizer on an unsuspecting Friday night back in Raleigh. Stories, laughter, and homemade chocolate martinis were the kick-off to a private party run by what looked like the Lebanese mafia at happy hour. After shots of Petron and running into people we didn't like from the old school--sore from fake smiling and conversational head nodding--we were off to the club where we danced the night away in a cloud of fog, sweat, and techno music.

The whole time I was thinking to myself how I hardly ever had nights like that. I lived a life that most people who work nine to five would only dream of by pursuing my artistic aspirations in the Big Apple. But little did they know that I would have given anything for just a little taste of their stability.

Making a career out of doing what you love often takes much of the fun out of doing it. What's worse is that--more than likely--you hardly ever get paid enough for it. The dancing taco promotional model and "Disco Dan" the sample-seller at checkout lines was hardly a career path worth bragging about. But all the books told us actors to keep doing "creative" work while going after our dreams. I didn't see how passing out glow pens for a major pharmaceutical company was helpful for my chances of working on Broadway; besides the fact that we were in Times Square while doing it.

Don't get me wrong, I thanked God every day I had the chance to do what I loved, but nothing is ever what it looks like, nor what it's cracked up to be. My friends went to work Monday through Friday and hated their jobs but worked hard at it and partied their asses off on the weekends because they could afford to do so. I, on the other hand, barely got by with enough to eat and danced my ass off every day in class so that I could audition for summer stock productions in the Catskills. The sacrifices one makes to follow a dream can be frighteningly all-encompassing.

It's awfully discouraging when you see people around you with nice clothes and weekend stories of vacationing to exotic places. You want to be happy for them, but one look at the amount of money you have in your bank account sucks all the joy you have right out of the picture. Still, every morning I'd hold my audition book tightly in my arms, flush the urinal a few times so I could get in a few lip trills before it was my turn to hit the high Gs. I popped my hips for another callback to play a dancing fork in Bristol, Pennsylvania's regional production of *Beauty and the Beast*. "We'll give it another year," I'd say. "If that doesn't work, I'm moving to Peru and becoming a tour guide at Machu Picchu."

At the club, Athena and I danced the night away. She kept taking breaks to meet her adoring fans, while I danced alone with a pole in the middle of the room. The air was sultry and there was a drunken haze that hovered over everyone in the room. While my gaydate was gone, a young woman took it upon herself to make her move, and in my drunken stupor she jumped on top of me from out of nowhere. I remembered hitting the floor rather hard on my knees, but thank God she broke my fall, because I didn't have any health insurance and a trip to the emergency room was not in the cards any time soon.

I helped her up, as any good Southern boy would, and tried to redeem myself the best I could. Unfortunately, a few good ol' boys had already shaken their cans of Pabst Blue Ribbon and poured the remaining contents over my head in disgrace. I saw Athena heading toward me, so I abruptly traded in my broke-down Chevy for a young, trendy Asian model.

After that, we drove to Athena's house and sang loud harmony in her car, just as we did in high school. With the windows rolled down, we floated our arms in waves like birds in flight. She loaned me pink pajama bottoms and we rested together, safe and sound, on top of her goose feather comforter with the matching pillow set. I didn't notice her snoring this time, but she did jab at my "Darth Vader" breathing and incessant twitching throughout the night. We left her house around 10 a.m. that Saturday and got breakfast at our favorite fast-food joint. Any self-respecting Southerner knows which one I'm referring to. Walking in, it smelled like grease and fried chicken. I was in Heaven!

The woman at the front register muffled while looking at her computer screen:

"Heler. Umm Buneeta. Wewcom ter Bojangles. Can ah take yer ORDER?"

"Hello…um, Buneta…I'd like a sausage biscuit, picnic fries, and a sweet tea."

"Do chwuuuut nayooo?"

"Umm…I would like a sausage biscuit, picnic fries, and a sweet tea, please."

"I heeerd ju. Ah was tawkin to da ga in da dravthrew. Do chwuuut nayoo?"

I stood there as Buneta entered into the cash register both of our orders with her extra-long fingernails, while proceeding to wipe her glistening, charcoal braids out of her eyes and squinted at the numbers that kept popping up on the screen. "Howd up, gimme uh secun…"

"Owkey, dattle be fowteen nanny nan. Drav up to da neux winder, pleez."

I puttered down the line to watch the food being served through the display window, as if I was the one in the drive through. I was so fixated on trying to understand her that I totally forgot where I was.

"Howd up…whey yoo gerin? Yoo gotta pay. Dattle be ate fowtee tharee."

I handed her what I thought was eight dollars and forty-three cents and she took it from me with a smack of her gum and a lazy wink. I noticed she was missing a few teeth but the one that was housed in the front of her gums was capped in gold and had writing on it. Upon further inspection, I realized that "Buneta" was indeed her real name.

"Thank yer. Hav uh nas der nah!"

"You too, Buneta."

"Awrite nah! Ya her?"

Athena and I listened to show tunes the entire way to the beach. We spoke about life, time, and how we had hoped the rain would subside long enough for us to catch some sun. When we got there, it was drizzling and cold, unheard of for mid-August weather in North Carolina. We laid our blanket down on the sand that felt more like wet concrete than anything soft or inviting and watched the waves curl on the beach devoid of fun-seekers and sun-tanning beach babes.

I looked up at the sky and mockingly exhaled, "Oh God, could anything else go wrong right now?" Just then, the drops of rain became fatter and more numerous. The seagulls that were flying over our heads ducked under us for cover. I could have sworn I heard one of them squawk, "Dumb asses!"

Even so, we decided to stay on the beach and enjoy our little vacation. We wrapped ourselves in the "Wildcats" afghan my mom was forced to buy from a choir fundraiser my junior year and used the beach towels to cover both of our legs and feet. The storm raged until we got hungry again and chose to skedaddle.

We grabbed lunch at this trendy Tex-Mex place that had killer salsa and I showed her around the town where I lived for a time with my best friend, Rachel. I knew the area because I had gone to school in Wilmington one summer to take a few extra credits in to graduate from NC State on time. We made our way down Market Street with most of our hair blowing in the salty breeze. There was a little museum off one of the roads, so we stopped in for a peek. It was a little hole-in-the-wall place dedicated to trolls. It kinda freaked us out (to be honest with you) but I rather enjoyed that kind of thing. Athena was pulled in through the rickety screened door against her better judgement.

We looked around and Athena reached her hands through my arm and pulled me close to her, resting her head on my shoulder. All around us were trolls: little ones, big ones, cool ones, nerdy ones, pink ones, and green ones. They all looked at us with the kind of eyes that whispered childhood nightmares right back into our consciousness. Just then an old lady crawled out of a backroom that was boarded up by planks of wood and started to speak to us in a groggy voice that made us duck for cover. We put our hands over each other's mouth and heard her have a conversation with herself.

"Heeeellllloooo? Is anyooooon there? Heeeellooo? Hello? HELLO? Hmm...I guess no one's there. Hellooo? Hello? Hmm...I guess there isn't anyone there. Ah, well. HELLO?"

Just then, a single cat meowed from the back room and one more followed suit.

"Okay, kitties...I'm coming!"

A herd of cats began to whine from beneath the floorboards and the old woman slunk back into the backroom to get a saucer of milk with the kind of limp that only Igor from the movie *Frankenstein* could pull off. We left as silently as we could, not to ruffle any crazy-lady feathers, and floored it out of the gravel parking lot toward downtown.

The rain had subsided when we reached the boardwalk. It was about two or so in the afternoon and the sun was just about to peek its head out from under the clouds. We had an absolute blast walking around town. We walked into shops and boutiques like we owned the place, asked very personal questions of a man behind the counter at a tattoo-parlor about various and sundry piercings, tried on the hottest pair of expensive jeans I've ever seen at an overpriced clothing store, and tasted a few too many free samples of ice cream at the local sweetshop.

We realized that if we were going to stay in Wilmington for another night we would need some clothes, because all we brought were bathing suits and towels. There was only so much one could do with a make-shift Mickey Mouse sarong and a rainbow lei. What was supposed to be a daytrip was quickly turning into a weekend getaway.

Next, we stopped off at the theatre that I had performed the musical version of *Chicago* in and inquired about any shows currently in production. I could feel this wasn't going to be a good idea, because no one spoke too highly about it, but we still felt compelled to buy tickets anyway. By this time, it was approaching 7:30 p.m. and we had to get some clothes if we were going to go to the show and find a club or a bar to pillage that evening.

We went to Marshalls. I found my sexy jeans and a hot pair of Calvin Klein briefs in less than ten minutes for under $20. I used a gift card to purchase it that I'd been saving since Christmas. It was exactly forty cents under the limit, and I gave the rest of the card to Athena so that I could change my clothes in the dressing room. She complained about not having any make-up to accentuate her vivacious personality.

We changed into our clothes and got in free to see the show thirty minutes late. After using a pair of scissors to cut the bottom of my new pants during intermission to fit the length of my dancing legs, we left after the first few songs of the second act and laughed the whole walk to my car. We drove to downtown Wilmington again and tried to find parking but ended up going to this swanky place to order martinis and an artisanal cheese plate. Athena ordered a chocolate martini, and I ordered a dirty one, just because I liked saying, "I'll take it up and dirty, please!"

When we arrived at the bar, we met a young man named David. We all danced and then decided to go to a nice, secluded spot on the beach for a skinny-dipping adventure in the ocean that night. It was around 3 a.m. when we got there, and I had my clothes off before the blanket hit the sand. I ran in and David soon followed. I waited and yelled to Athena to join us, but the waves kept taking us farther and farther away and I eventually lost sight of her. When David had had enough, I floated on my back staring up at the moon and starry sky with my genitals flopped to one side and my toes bobbing up and down with the waves.

I made my way to the shore and walked onto the sand like I was wearing a fine, tailor-made suit. I walked past a few nighttime beach goers and calmly said, "Hello" like we were next-door neighbors when they shined their flashlights at me for much longer than was necessary. I inquired if any of them had seen a tall gay man and a short Asian woman nearby. They proceeded to chuckle uncomfortably, so I decided to keep walking toward any sort of civilization I could find in the darkness of night. Athena had fallen asleep, and it was time for us all to hit the hay.

David offered us his place and we accepted knowing full well it was either that or sleeping in my car for the rest of the morning. It afforded us the luxury of a shower and a bathroom, couches, blankets, and the all-important air-conditioning unit. We met his dog Kaire, which I thought was a gorgeous name. I read a few excerpts from a coffee table book dedicated to the sordid lives and tell-all-tales of retired porn stars. I didn't know quite what to make of it except for the fact that David knew most of their work by rote. I put the book down and started leafing through *Webster's Dictionary* to pretend I wasn't a complete pervert. We played with his roommate's cat with an automated light toy and drove her crazy when she realized she could never catch the damn thing.

After a hardy breakfast at Chick-Fil-A, we were off by 9 a.m. that Sunday morning and headed straight for the beach once more. The sun was shining, the sand was hot between our toes, and the ocean looked divine. The only people there were the locals, so we didn't have to deal with the usual bridge and tunnelers.

Athena and I spread lotion over our glistening skin and laid down basking in the salty air and joyous screams of happy children and playful lovers. We listened to music, talked about anything that popped into our minds, and played in the waves together all afternoon. Since we forgot to bring water, we were in the final stages of dehydration when we decided to head back to the car. Our bodies wouldn't let us get any further, so we stopped and shared a bottle of water and a pink lemonade icee to quench our thirst.

Around 2 p.m. that afternoon we stopped at a Wendy's for lunch. Then, hit the road again listening to the same tunes we did on the way to the beach and still talking about the craziest stuff that we could think of.

Dreamgirls blasted from my low-quality speakers as our beach vacation drifted out of sight in the rear-view mirror. We were exhausted and sad to have to say goodbye to such an amazing adventure. I knew that it was going to be our last trip to the beach together, and I was sure that weekend would be worth remembering for many years to come.

The Kings of Creek Ridge

The ride back was the only time I let myself cry the entire trip. I was navigating in the passenger's seat, hiding behind glassy eyes, while my little brother (the husband to be) was driving his two best friends back to their homes. Everyone was hung over, tired and wanting to get back to their normal lives, but the closer we got to our destinations the quieter we all became, and the more we wished we could go back to our palace in the mountains.

I grew up as a city boy in the South. Before this trip, I'd never been camping. My family's idea of roughing it out in nature was pulling off I-95 on our way to New York to catch a few winks in a McDonald's parking lot. I was never taught how to be a man, but I always had friends who could touch their toes and leap into sporadic song at the drop of a hat. So, when I found out that I was responsible for planning and executing a fun-filled bachelor party weekend for a bunch of beer-guzzling soccer studs, you can imagine my initial trepidation.

It was August, and we all met at Erik and Stephanie's apartment on a Thursday afternoon. The plan was that I'd supply the guys with enough alcohol and buffalo wings to feed an entire army. In exchange, they agreed to have a good time and eventually pass out within the allotted rectangles I demarcated with electric tape along the floor. This way, if their nametags remained intact, I could tell them apart the next morning when I had to drag their lifeless corpses into the two vehicles that would safely take them to the mountains.

Of course, it didn't happen the way I expected at all; I suppose, nothing worthwhile ever does. Yet, in the long run it all worked out just fine. They finished all the food and I lost track of the empty beer cans I picked up that were precariously thrown about the room.

Everything went smoothly and after a while there was no more need for the glow tape and first aid kit I had stashed away in the medicine cabinet. In fact, we ended up playing an entire game of capture the flag that lasted well into the morning on the campus of NC State. I felt like a total boy for the first time in a long time.

I was apprehensive about the idea of playing a sport involving physical contact without mandatory rules in place to avoid unnecessary trips to the emergency room. However, the game went well, and we all drove back to the apartment for a few hours of sleep.

On Friday morning, Stephanie and I planned the beginnings of a road-game we decided to call "The Hunt." Stephanie was Erik's fiancée and my only saving grace around all that bubbling testosterone.

Now, all it was was sort of a scavenger hunt, but you couldn't call it that in front of those types of guys. I mean these were the types of guys who used to throw bananas at me in the cafeteria, the real green ones that sting when they hit plump, unexpecting flesh. So, I knew I had to keep my mouth shut and legs uncrossed for as long as I could stand it.

It meant survival for me. But--more importantly--it meant that my little brother would have the best weekend of his life, if I had anything to say about it. That was of utmost importance, since I was the best man, and it was my solemn duty to properly bid singledom a fond farewell for the man of the hour. After all, he was my childhood best friend and now he was off to start a family of his own. It was just something I had to do well for so many reasons.

We divided ourselves into teams to play a short clue game that Stephanie created. I'd never known a woman so dedicated to creating family-friendly experiences before. She had placed the clue in a jar at the bottom of the neighborhood swimming pool: the first to find it won a five-minute head start. We jumped in our cars and began the race toward the finish line while completing as many tasks as possible that were written on "The Hunt" list. We had to take pictures of each task along the way to the mountains and would eventually meet up at a place called "Harper's II," which was a car wash in Greensboro.

I made the boys give Ronald McDonald a lap dance, pick a fellow team member's nose, and try to wake up a dead animal on the side of the road. They had to moon a car full of old people, give a law enforcement officer a piggyback ride, and ask random people for money to help pay for our make-believe hamster's heart transplant.

It's amazing how soon people part with their money when an animal or small child is mentioned in the brief. No one really questioned our integrity, so accepting money from strangers was easier than we thought. Altogether, we made about eighty-four cents, hardly enough to pay for the gauze needed for such an intricate surgical procedure.

Next, I had the guys go to an adult sex shop and buy Erik a tasteless piece of pornographic material. Consequently, we all received much more than we bargained for. There was a great deal of information about things we always had questions about, so it was interesting to see how many of our sexual lives paralleled no matter what our vast differences in taste were. I felt like an ambassador for women when talking to these unassuming boys.

We learned the benefits of glass verses rubber dildos and how to relax an abnormally tight Kegel muscle. It was slightly awkward being the only gay guy in the group, but I was beginning to know them a little more intimately, so I had high hopes for the coming mountain-weekend adventure.

There's no denying the fact that those types of stores are intimidating, but the woman behind the counter was very helpful and made all of us promise to return. Only next time, I was going to come alone or with a boyfriend if I could help it. With a wink at the woman behind the register, we parted ways, leaving behind a trail of glorious machismo.

I had the boys fake a seizure in a public place, perform a "Chinese fire drill" at a busy intersection, and ask a homeless person for their autograph. However, nothing could have prepared us for what was in store while getting an exotic car wash at Harper's II. I had never been to a strip club or had ever gotten my car washed by anyone who wasn't thoroughly clothed at the time, so the anticipatory dry heaves, wet belches, and butterflies in the pit of the stomach were par for the course.

I felt like I was going in for a simultaneous colonoscopy and root canal procedure. I was fighting the feeling of fleeing immediate danger, because I didn't want to embarrass myself in front of these kinds of guys. I just wanted to lay low for a while and not have to be the big, best man with expectations and all. So, when we came around the corner of the car wash and saw what it was all about, I breathed a heavy sigh and took my seat at the table with the rest of the "gentlemen."

These girls had breasts that looked more like overly ripe avocados and stomachs lined with stretch marks that an entire fleet of ships could easily navigate in the harshest of weather. Thankfully, they shaved their pubic areas, but what was left were little red razor bumps that accentuated their genital rashes and the track marks on their thighs.

These ladies had names like "Veronica" and "Venus," but looked more like "Delores" and "Ester Mae" from some trailer park near Louisburg. I did get to witness one attractive light-skinned African American woman give a fat Mexican man a lap dance in something called THE PRIVATE ROOM. I even learned a few moves from my obstructed observations. While the other boys were gawking at Venus, I had one eye in the private room and the other on my car.

Just then, I saw a patrol car pull up, and five cops hopped out to take their seats at the empty table marked "reserved." I quickly realized whom I'd be fighting within the system if my car got scratched and I tried to sue the place. So, I shut up and took a swig of my warm beer and watched the dim lights flicker off the broken bits of an old disco ball.

I'd eke out a smile and a head nod every time the boys got excited by receiving a wink from one of the ladies. I think it was just soap in their eyes, but I thought I'd let them feel like kings for a while. Then, we made a mad dash into our cars to stay on track and headed down I-40W for another couple of hours until we saw the Earth begin to ascend into the clouds, as we traveled deeper and deeper into the heart of western North Carolina.

After getting lost a few times and completing all but one of the road games tasks, my team finally reached the campsite first. Erik wanted rustic, and that's exactly what he got. The company I contracted supplied us with logs for fire, but if you wanted to take a shower or use the bathroom, you'd better put on your hiking boots, dig a ditch and poop, or feel comfortable bathing with the trout in the river. I was down for anything new and exciting since I had brought extra toilet paper and unscented bug spray in my plastic duffle bag from The Gap.

When we got to the campsite at Creek Ridge, we saw that there were two covered shelters, and they were just above a flowing creek. The view was simply breathtaking! The sounds of running water and the cricks and cracks of breaking branches in the woods was enough to make me marvel at what I had been missing for so many years. The boys knew what they had to do from their many years of fine Southern upbringing: set up shelter, make a fire, and drink beer; not necessarily in that order, of course. I, on the other hand, was more interested in exploring this newfound territory that I had never had the privilege of experiencing before. So, while they were pitching tents, I wondered around the woods for a while.

We had arrived around 7 p.m., so I took it upon myself to start cooking the food before it got too dark. The fire was almost out by the time all of us were shit-faced drunk, trying to sit still on unstable beer coolers and falling headfirst into large rocks. A select few of us were nudged inside those tailgating chairs you get free from the supermarket if you accumulate enough bonus points at the checkout line. Some of the guys were placing small pouches between their lower lips and gums. I asked what they were doing, and they offered me a chance to try it.

With a sly smirk and no explanation, they gave me a little bit and I slowly placed it in my mouth. I felt like my old geometry teacher, Mr. Irwin, the day after he ate fish that he knew he was allergic to. My lip became engorged with blood and felt numb. It was uncomfortable, and I did the best I could not to swallow any of the stingy, putrid, mint-flavored juice. I was already drunk, so the high from chewing tobacco hit me like a ton of bricks.

I kept it in for as long as I could, but eventually spit it out without anyone noticing. I staggered and wavered from side to side for a while, and eventually got up knowing I was going to vomit. And hurl I did, right into the hollow of a tree that sat beneath one of the shelters. I decided to fall asleep next to my biodegradable barf-bag, but one of the boys took me over his shoulders and put me in Erik's tent. I tossed and turned all night and woke up with the birds.

The next morning, I zipped my way out of the tent for some fresh air and sunlight. It was unbelievable! I had never felt so close to nature as I did at that moment. I looked up and saw nothing but green leaves and branches covering us in a blanket of splendor and safety.

Surprisingly, I wasn't hung-over, so I felt perfectly fine walking down to the creek with a shampoo bottle and some face soap contemplating whether I should take off my clothes, knowing full well the boys were comatose by that hour. I looked around to see if anyone would notice me disrobing from the other campsites. I then took off one article of clothing at a time and put a beach towel around my naughty bits.

I dipped my feet in the cold running water and felt the dirt and grit between my toes on the creek bed. It felt amazing! I drew the towel up from my shins one inch at a time, as I descended into the water, and eventually threw it on a big rock near where I entered the stream. I felt like I was home, like I was living in some fantastic '80s movie being lifted into the air by a svelte Patrick Swayze.

After bathing for a bit, I gathered my things, put my towel back on, and got dressed to cook breakfast for the fellows. By this time, it was about 8 a.m. and the smell of eggs and sausage was wafting through the air. One by one, the guys started waking up like bumbling bears. Maybe it was the sound of me picking up empty beer cans that woke them up, but I like to imagine it was the smell of a home-cooked meal that aroused them from their slumbers.

The boys devoured their meal in almost complete silence, as I finished my duties as den mother, and sat in one of the folding chairs making sure I'd be ready in case one of them needed the Heimlich. They talked about fond memories, past athletic wins and losses, and how "totally gay" people were for not knowing what a "buck shot" was. I just sat back and wondered what planet I was on and just what the hell a buck shot really was.

It was Saturday, and we scheduled a white-water rafting trip in the afternoon that we couldn't be late for or else we'd lose our deposit. After shooting the shit for a few hours, the boys went off to swim in the wading pool downstream. A few other guys went in search of more firewood. Even though we had plenty enough as it was, it made them feel more like men to use sharp, heavy objects. And I was happy to know that we were all preoccupied.

I stayed to clean up the trash and tied it in small, round bundles for easy disposal, not fully appreciated by the other boys who simply used them as makeshift seats. After I was done, I found myself alone again at the campsite. I was antsy, so I went down to the mouth of the creek and found a rock big enough to sit on. I started a few sun salutations and ended up practicing yoga for about an hour and a half. A few of the boys were on the upstream side of the river. Danny caught a small fish and held it with his two fingers to show me. As they came around the bend, they saw me balancing on a rock in nothing but a navy-blue swimsuit.

I don't know if I freaked them out, because they paused for a moment, but my concentration was so fixed on what I was doing that I didn't care. They kept going and appeared to try not to disturb me, which I thought was kind. Balancing on a rock in the middle of a running river and falling off my tiny perch could have had devastating consequences.

The afternoon sun was appearing above the trees. Rays of light were shining through the branches and were driving into the ground like intangible beams of radiant heat. When no one was looking I ran through them like a little girl through a sprinkler, letting the light warm and tickle my manicured toes. Everyone returned to the campsite wet and was excited about the rest of the day. So, we decided to go into the village to gather much-needed materials and grab lunch. I couldn't even think about drinking anymore alcohol, but the idea of having someone else cook a meal to feed these hungry beasts was the most pleasurable suggestion I'd heard all morning.

We found a place called Hiker's Knob and sat down in the back of the restaurant for service. It took them an hour to get our food. We ended up taking most of it to go and scarfing down the rest. Pickiness wasn't something I had to worry about with these guys but procuring a full supply of food and beer was always in the back of my mind.

We got to the rafting place with fifteen minutes to spare. After a few unpleasant moments involving an angry woman with a bad dye job, we received our lifejackets and white helmets for our river excursion. Our guide was named Will, and he was just as manly and knowledgeable about the outdoors as the other guys in our boat. I felt horribly out of place and wanted desperately to fall off the side of the boat like Goldie Hawn in *Overboard*, crying "Arturo…Arturo!" Sadly, no one there would have jumped in to save me or understood the reference.

Of course, I knew nothing of what anyone was talking about, so I quietly nodded my head and sat in the back to paddle. Our lifejackets smelled like Fritos and wet dog, our helmets chafed the tips of our ears, and were probably infested with lice. But it was all part of the "great outdoors" experience, so I went along with it like a fish out of water.

We had an absolute blast! The whole experience was both serene and exhilarating all at the same time. When we weren't working together to get through a rapid, we were coasting down the river admiring the hills, crests, and trees that lined our view. It was majestic and utterly exquisite.

We were sharing the trip with a church group from somewhere in Virginia, so one could make a safe bet that we would be the rowdy ones that afternoon. We yelled across the water, pulled each other into the mucky waves, and laughed out loud when someone fell over like prep-school boys. We splashed each other with playful banter like a one of those romantic, vintage, gay films, and aggressively competed to be the first to cross the finish line.

By that afternoon, I had gotten a little sick of all the masculine energy and wanted to go back to the campsite with a few of the other fellows who just wanted to drink. The rest went and jumped off a cliff. I didn't know if I was perturbed by all the incessant ball scratching or the constant gay jokes, but the fact that every woman who happened to walk by was "the hottest girl" they had seen all day was starting to get to me.

I had also never heard so many guys fart or talk about poop to such a degree and depth before in my entire life. Granted, I hadn't played many sports and I spent most of my life growing up at church, transfixed in front of a television, or at a piano with my metronome providing a consistent, dependable beat. I couldn't get over the fact that these guys thought they were the hottest shit on the planet and their bravado was bugging me. I started feeling horrible for their girlfriends. I had to get away for a while and have some alone time to reconnect with the spiritual forces emanating from my current surroundings, present company excluded.

There were two boys of every name, which I thought was hilarious. There were two Eriks, two Dans, there were supposed to be two Mikes--but our older brother bailed, per usual--two Drews, and two twins. The Drews and I went to this greasy mountain diner that had been around since lard was law of the land. It was called Black Mountain Restaurant. I had the grilled chicken salad and was scared to see what their version of "Cajun spices" was. One Drew got the steak, and the other Drew got the burger, both well done and plain. After dinner, we returned to the campsite. I had to go out for a solo hike to clear my mind.

Drew gave me a flashlight and told me how to shake it if it started to dwindle and the other Drew wished me luck and told me not to get lost or die. I thought that was sweet coming from him. There was still some light out when I started my trek, but I soon lost the trail and decided to jump some rocks in the river to get further downstream toward my intended destination. I remembered there was a wading pool that the other boys visited early in the day while I was upside-down on a rock practicing my down-dog. So, I went to check it out.

I leapt from rock to rock with dance-like precision. As soon as I reached my spot atop a cliff overlooking the pool under a raging waterfall, I sat in half lotus and began to meditate. I closed my eyes and didn't open them until night had fallen. I lost track of time, but it seemed like hours had gone by, so I immediately got myself a stick and shook the flashlight on to head back to camp.

Along the way it was too dark to see anything, so I ended up falling into the raging water when I missed a step leading into a grand jeté. Holding my flashlight high above my head, I tugged at my walking stick to help me get back to land safely. When no rock was in sight, I rushed the river bottom and swam my way upstream, flashing my light a few inches in front of me to see where I was headed. I felt like Rambo, wielding a rainbow-colored sash and a temperamental flashlight instead of a machete.

I saw the glow of a campfire in the distance and directed my feet toward the light as the current drifted me downstream. Oddly enough, I saw a man not much older than I was hitting his head against the trunk of a tree. The action wasn't violent by any means but more of a flagellation of some kind. Not even registering that this man could very well be off his rocker, I inquired if he was all right and if he could direct me to the trail back up the mountain. With the glow of the fire from his eyes, I could tell that this guy had some serious issues that I wasn't going to get involved in if I could help it.

After inviting me to join him on a nearby log, he gave me the necessary information I needed to begin my journey back to camp. I bid him a polite farewell and a quick "best of luck."

"Wait, have you given any thought about saving your immortal soul?" he asked.

I ran up the mountain with the kind of animalistic fervor one would see on *The Biggest Loser*, high-tailed it past the pine-straw heaps and lunged over boulders in order to find the trail in the pitch-black forest night.

I'm sure the idea of me dying in the woods in the dark would have created quite a panic from the other boys. Come to find out when I reached the site, hardly anyone knew I was gone. When I got back, Danny had cooked the hotdogs and leftover hamburgers, and everyone was drinking a beer and relaxing. I quietly sunk into the group like I had been there the whole time, grabbing a seat on one of the coolers and popping open an ice-cold Busch Light. I was just happy to be in the company of anyone remotely resembling normal.

Erik made a toast to one of his friends who had recently passed away. There was a moment of silence and I was grappling with what kind of toast I would provide my little brother on his bachelor's weekend. I made sure enough time had gone by and that everyone had a drink in their hand and made a short, but well-devised off-the-cuff speech to Erik and his blessed future with his soon-to-be wife. My speech was accepted by the rest of the men and one of the Drews handed me a cigar in congratulations. I declined, recalling the smell of vomit on my breath from the chewing tobacco incident the night before. I waved smoky embers out of my face, as I moved closer to the hypnotic flames of the fire.

A young hippie couple stopped by and asked us for a flashlight to return up the mountain to get their car for a trip into the village. We gave it to them, and the young man offered us a "nugget." He then picked out a clump of marijuana from a contact lens case and placed it lovingly into my open palm. Overjoyed, but trying to conceal my excitement, I asked if anyone had anything to smoke it out of. One of the boys made a makeshift beer can-pipe. After the night I had, I would have smoked a forest if it meant I'd fall asleep faster.

The campfire was beautiful. It was golden, yellow, orange with red flames surrounding a blue and white center. As the night wore on, trash was thrown into the fire to keep it nice and hot. The idea of burning things was a Southern thing, and so I was trying to pick cans and plastic from the fire so they could be recycled properly. There was a green glow off the Bud Light box and there were a few moments where I thought I saw purple emanate from one of the empty Busch cans. I could have just been intoxicated, or high, but after a while the fire died down and so did my desire to stay up all night.

I went to sleep with the other smart ones, while the Eriks, Toms, and twins stayed up celebrating their last night in the mountains. I couldn't sleep a wink, I thought the weed would have helped, but the sounds of the boys frolicking were the only obstacle to my dreamy bliss. Their cries of joy made me happy, but I kept silently wishing that lightning would strike them before I got to the ax lodged in the tree beside them. The madness ended just before the sun rose. Then, the biggest bee I'd ever seen made its way into our tent. I literally screamed bloody murder.

I got out, checking all my appendages and most of my holes, and went about my morning ritual sans yoga. It was my last time bathing in the creek with the fish. I finished drying off when I started to see several steady drops of rain fall on my pale skin. I noticed the raging water was higher than the previous morning, and that this time the water wasn't clear; it was more of a muddy brown color. The runoff from the rainstorm upstream was making its way down to our campsite.

I didn't have to wake the men up because their damp sleeping bags did that for me. I watched under the tarp and waited for the ensuing madness to occur with a Grinch-like anticipation. Much like I had woken up the boys in my tent with a shrill of fear from a flying bumblebee, the boys began to scream at the thought of their electrical equipment getting wet.

Like popcorn, they sprang up out of their tents, and came over to meet the rest of us under the tarp. They began to run around to save all their lanterns and expensive GPS systems from the torrential downpour, while we watched the campsite turn into a swampy mess in a matter of minutes. It would have been a shitty way to end our adventure, but I was determined not to let that happen.

We got all our stuff together and headed up the trail to meet the owner with his four-wheeler and cargo trailer. I asked Bob if he needed some extra weight upfront to give the vehicle more traction since it was still raining a little and the ground was completely soaked. I helped the boys load and lug their stuff, and then waited until all the gear was up at the dock. I jumped on the front of the bike and headed up the trail with my legs dangling in front of the wheels. It was a completely terrifying but exhilarating experience!

Eventually, we all got up the mountain and packed the trucks for the trip home. We met at the Black Mountain Restaurant for breakfast and most of us went to the Hot Springs Spa for a hot, relaxing, mineral-water bath. We got there and read a sign that said, "Established in 1790." We were shocked and couldn't believe that this place had been around for so long.

They took us to a waiting bath. It was just a Jacuzzi tub that sat about four to six comfortably, but we managed to squeeze in eight or nine uncomfortably and still had a good time. I can only imagine what gunk my pores must have soaked in from these rough-and-tumble kind of guys, but we all sat and chatted, relaxed, and commented on our trip like old men in a hot sauna talking about the good old days. Pecs, bellies, chicken legs and body hair were all that was visible above the steamy foam. It was a nice bonding experience, but I felt that we all wanted to get back to our normal lives as soon as possible.

After the bath, we headed into our vehicles and followed each other with militaristic precision down the road until we eventually lost sight when the cars split off the highway in different directions. One of the Drews mentioned that we should play the letter game and they had to explain it to me rather slowly until I caught on. We all sang songs on the radio, eventually getting quiet when the mountains disappeared and all we could see was the flat open road in front of us.

I did a lot of soul searching that weekend and made a vow that I would return to the mountains again someday. I had never felt so close to nature in all my life, and it was almost as if time had stopped for a few days when I was with those boys. I sat there watching my little brother drive. He looked at me a few times during the ride back and we connected eyes once that I can remember vividly and smiled. Without saying a word, he showed me how thankful he was to have had the best weekend of his life, and to have a brother like me there to share it with.

I gazed back with much older eyes and said the same thing without needing to find the right words. I looked out the passenger seat window and felt the wind rustle my hair and slide up and over my forehead. I leaned back and started to think about our childhood together: building forts with nothing but sheets and couch cushions, riding bikes together, and watching his games from the sidelines. That Thanksgiving turkey and the time we ran down the stairs on Christmas morning to see what Santa had brought us. I used to get so irritated when he'd follow me around everywhere, and I was jealous that so many of my guy friends ended up liking him more than me when we were young because I was never good at guy stuff. Now, I was just hoping he would be my shadow one last time.

I remembered the first time I'd ever seen him drunk. I got him up on stage and we sang harmony alongside one another under smoky, green strobe lights. Then, there was the time the comedian called me out at that comedy club for my undeniable lisp. But the greatest memory of all was teaching him how to dance for his wedding. That I was never going to forget.

I guess my time with the Kings of Creek Ridge wasn't all that bad. It brought my brother and I a little closer after so many years apart. It got us both thinking about what's important in life and how precious love, friends, and family really are. How time and love compete for our attention and give us all something to live and strive for. In any case, I shared an unbelievable four days with men who gave me a lot to think about. Maybe one day soon I'll understand it all a bit better.

My Columbus Day Esca-Parade!

Having come home to Harlem after parading around Fifth Avenue in a shiny metal helmet with a sharp dagger by my side, I made my way to the kitchen for a much-needed snack. It was dinnertime and the fruit flies were getting more to eat than I was. I reached into my pocket and pulled out the hundred-dollar bill I was paid for services rendered at the Columbus Day parade. I headed to La Posada to get guacamole, salsa, and chips to go. It was the least I could do to treat myself after a long day of ego-bruising.

I always thought Columbus Day was one of those holidays that everyone pretends doesn't exist, like Flag Day or Singles Awareness Day. If you aren't mandated to dress up or drink heavily Americans usually brush it off as just another day off. But the parade, which I thought would be attended by a couple of tourists, turned out to be a regular episode from the *Sopranos*. Tony would breathe fire and dance inside a twenty-foot balloon rolled violently down the street by a handful of out-of-work actors like myself.

It reminded me of the Gay Pride parade, but with more repression, back hair, and Vitalis oozing onto the streets in slippery puddles. We would be marching behind the New York City police department on horseback, so I had to watch my step in every sense of the word.

I woke up that morning at 6:30 a.m. to make it down to east 69th street by 8 a.m. Winter was coming, and I was five minutes late, so I sprinted the rest of the way in thermal undergarments. I had no expectations except for the fact that I was going to be paid in cash and on time, which was a welcome treat. I entered through the ground floor of the Columbus Foundation and was greeted by three huge men with perfect hairlines and a combined cholesterol level that far exceeded the elevator capacity of such a lavish establishment.

No one had any idea who I was or why I was there, but having been through that drill a number of times while auditioning, I quietly sat on a ledge by the buffet table and waited for someone to come find me. I prepared my flawless alibi. "Oh no, I wasn't late...I've been here the whole time finding my inner soldier. Please, I need my space."

The message Sue left on the phone indicated that I was going to be playing the part of a soldier in The Gumba Club's Roman Legion. My password was "Roman" (very hush-hush) and that I was to be working for a man named "Alfred" (again...very hush-hush). It was like something out of a *Batman* movie. So naturally I was intrigued when Alfred came down the stairs wearing a white sash proclaiming "President of the Parade" in chancery font.

I thought I was going to meet Batman's butler, or at least a crippled old man in a chair stroking a lap cat and audibly breathing through a tube! Who the hell was this guy in a salmon-colored suit with a Boehner spray tan? I was already longing to leave but could smell delicious food stewing in the kitchen, so I acquiesced to the powers that be and reluctantly did as I was told.

Just then, the cater-waiters opened the gold lids covering the buffet table and before I could count to "Guido" the table had been stripped of all chicken parms, prosciutto, and breadsticks. All that was left were some greasy sausages and a few packets of artificial sweeteners. But I'd had to work with less before. "Who wants Sugar Flavored Water and casse-croûte de saucisse?"

We then made our way up a red-carpeted staircase with gold-plated railings toward a ballroom that smelled like Pine Sol and fresh-baked lemon squares. It was dark at first, but when someone reached the light switch the room seemed to illuminate rather than just simply light up, as if flipping a switch was too mundane in a room with a crested ceiling, marble floor, Swiss woodcarvings, and etched pillars imported from Spain.

We sat down slowly as if to preserve the sordid history of the plush, red chairs. Honestly, we didn't want to break anything for fear of having to pay for it or find ourselves whacked by the Mafia. The rest of the out-of-work actors and I sat in a concentric circle at the farthest table from the door in complete silence. Much like at auditions there was this inherent sense of competition and hierarchical camaraderie brewing, waging a silent war for the coveted position as "Featured Extra." Only this time, no one wanted to say anything because many of us had just woken up and still smelled like alcohol and stale pizza from the night before.

Eventually, the boys started conversing about things like non-union commercials and extra work on independent film sets. Things like who was the best and worst actors on the scene, the hottest actresses of all time, and what famous people they'd worked with so far in their wildly successful career as "Background-Artist Extraordinaire." I became bored rather quickly with the conversation, so I politely excused myself. I went to the next room to make a phone call to anyone who would pick up.

After a bit of time pretending to call people I didn't know; I heard a roar of laughter in the other room and realized I was ditching the "I Love Everything Italian" slide-show presentation. I quickly returned to my seat in the hopes they'd slip up and reveal where Jimmy Hoffa's body was stashed. I finally met up with my group that by this time had all been sleeping in puddles of their own saliva. We hopped into a private chartered bus to take us a few blocks down the street to the parade's starting point. A brisk walk in the crisp, October air was apparently against parade policy.

We met up with a guy who took us through blocked-off streets and flashed cards at police officers to allow safe passage while onlookers leaned in with eye and ear to find out if we were celebrities willing to take pictures with their offspring. It was a feeling I've had before coming out of the stage doors wearing the coveted "Talent" badge on tour in Las Vegas, but it hardly seemed warranted at this venture and time.

Then, an older gentleman, frail and sun-beaten, made his way out of another minivan where he had been living for over eleven years. He began tossing us costumes and dingy, metal weaponry that he rented out to events for his livelihood. He was one of those suppliers who rented costumes and props for Renaissance fairs and four-hour non-equity productions of *Hamlet* starring Mary Jane Doe and John Allen Smith, recently off tour with *Run Diego, Run* and *Sesame Street Live!*

I staggered off to the side of the crowd of unemployed actors and found my niche leaning against the old man's gray Dodge Caravan with "Wash Me" sadly finger-painted in dirt on the back window. He didn't have enough props for all of us, including me, who by this time had taken over the duties of costume mistress because Harry Carry kept handing out mismatched costumes and putting shin guards on the boys' forearms. When I was finished dressing the others, I searched the water-damaged cardboard box that held our costumes to find only a silver helmet and a gold belt buckle with a sheathed dagger.

We were suddenly whisked away down the street passing onlookers by the thousands. I felt stupid and out of place and hated every minute of it. Once again, another challenge I had dragged myself into for a measly hundred bucks that I desperately needed. I began second-guessing my purpose in life and the metaphysical existence of God.

The parade began after a lot of starting and stopping as horses dropped their loads along the path for tuxedoed men with pooper-scoopers and trash bags to cart away. It totally broke the tough, Roman soldier ambiance us actors were creating with the knowledge we had gained from our one-week Miesner intensive actors' training workshop. The fact that I was the only guy in the group with an oversized helmet, a tight "chain metal" thermal shirt, ripped blue jeans and a gold studded belt with a wimpy dagger ruined any chance of using this experience as a resume booster.

I could hear the crowd jeering in my head and prayed to God the bagpipers behind us weren't planning on blowing out the tune to the Village People's YMCA on my account. Every time I'd hear them play YANKEE DOODLE DANDY, I knew a few of their snickers would be for me. I smiled knowing full well what I was getting myself into. I took in the space as we rounded the first corner toward Fifth Avenue and looked down the straight, long road with a bite of my lip and my stomach tucked in, pushing my chest out to repel any rotted cabbage that might be hurled at my illustrious bosom. Thankfully, the helmet covered most of my face so there was no real threat to my career.

The first part was easy. No one ever watches from the start of the parade, except those who happen to be around Times Square and don't feel the urge to walk up a few blocks to a much nicer vantage point. Columbus Circle couldn't arrive soon enough. I breathed deep, trying to make manly conversation with the Greek god next to me and the tall, skinny model to my right in a red pageboy ensemble. All of us really wanted nothing to do with the whole humiliating experience so there was an unspoken camaraderie of sorts that made the entire event swing into a steady, rhythmic pulse.

One child loudly said to his mother, "Mommy that soldier has sneakers on!" The mother politely told her son that I was a “special soldier” and that I probably couldn't afford leather sandals on my soldier’s salary. “Hmm…clever,” I thought. A rather inebriated woman with sharp, pointy eyebrows blared from the sidelines: "Someone woke up late this morning and couldn't find his big sword!"
The crowd chortled in amusement. The sheer audacity and perfectly timed delivery grated over my freshly trimmed arm hairs so there wasn’t a chance in hell I could come back with a piqued enough remark without looking like a poor sport. So, I bit my lip. I bit it hard.

Then, a child squeaked, "Mommy, that soldier looks gay!" The middle-aged woman immediately stopped waving her miniature Italian American flag and covered her child's mouth. The crowd roared with laughter. She shushed the child and said, "No, baby there are no gay soldiers. That parade doesn't start for another nine months."

It suddenly felt easy to be laughed at. Once you've been outed by an eight-year-old in pigtails, you know the end is in sight. We came up to the last few stoplights and like a bad Rockettes’ concert we all turned our heads independently to face the camera. The young boy with Down’s Syndrome that had joined our ranks followed suit as we walked onto the red carpet that was promoting a pharmaceutical drug company sponsor at just the right angle to catch maximum airtime.

We finished the parade and took off our costumes by a row of stretch limousines. We were each handed our hundred-dollar bill and told to take a cab downtown to return our costumes. Of course, we’d have to all share cabs to keep most of our new earnings.

But wait! Where was the Down's Syndrome kid? Had we left him to fend for himself with those psychotic clowns on tricycles miming "happy" like convulsive, mental patients and the middle school marching bands behind us? Did we really let him carry the big sword this whole time without proper supervision? I almost forgot about little Jo-Jo whose mother sprayed water into his mouth from a plastic bottle every other block to prevent dehydration in the perfect, mild, fall weather while he continued unbuttoning his pants to expose himself to squirrels.

We were given twenty dollars to split between two cabs after a very hostile confrontation between the driver and our group leader. The all-powerful and egocentric Rolando hailed a third cab for himself with his own money as his personal chariot back to the foundation's headquarters. I emptied my various and sundries into the first car's trunk. I was given the option of sitting on Richard's lap, which I thankfully declined, taking a seat in the back of the comfy cab with the Mighty Rolando instead. "Seats taken," he jested. I could have punched him in his single dimple. I gave him a sideways squint and my best fake smile and told the cab driver to take us down to Park and 45th.

I made the trek across three avenues holding Rob's golden spear of the Sentinels and our shiny helmets hung loosely on my pointer finger. One really can't imagine how heavy things were in the centuries before modern comforts. Before our micro-suede couches and terrycloth robes, there was stone seating for two and a personal line of burlap sacks to tie twine around to attract prospective mates. If that didn't work, there was always a club to the head if advances weren't met. Many people still believe the whole Roman era was like something portrayed in a movie starring Russell Crowe or Angelina Jolie. Perhaps it was Meissner of me not to wear underwear that day after all?

"Yes, Mr. Lipton...I really felt connected to my character doing work on the Columbus Day Esca-Parade. It was important for me to dig deep and to get to know my inner soldier. Yes, the jeans and tennis shoes were somewhat of a distraction at times, but I just used that as fuel to delve right into the part and feel my character from the inside out."

"Did the thermal shirt help you in this discovery?"

"No, not so much...that was more of a bad wardrobe choice on my part, but nevertheless I thought my career really blossomed after that day. I mean, I started getting emails from casting agents begging me to come in and read for THIS project and THAT leading role. I just had to take it one day at a time, you know? Didn't want to explode on the scene too soon, you see."

"Yes, uh huh...uh huh" (nodding in agreement with hands clasped below the chin). "When did you first know that the role 'That Gay, Roman Soldier Guy' would launch you into national stardom?"

"I knew the moment I smelled that first giant horse turd that I had arrived! I had finally reached the pinnacle of my illustrious career. I heard people shouting and screaming in recognition from the fenced-off sidelines barricaded by police officials and I couldn't help but feel…validated! So, to answer your question, Mr. Lipton, I always knew I was destined for stardom. It just took a heap of horseshit and a lot of embarrassing failures to get me there."

The Smell of Success

After the parade, I promised myself I would try to avoid embarrassment like that again at all costs. But many times, the power of one's destiny takes precedence over their puny need to be liked by others. I realized a lot of what I was experiencing stemmed from a great many things that weren't being allowed to come to the surface.

One example was my countless attempts at appearing straight, which led me to the sport of running...away. My father was a track star in high school, and I grew up hearing his tales of heroism in the Heights. I, on the other hand, hid in the bathroom during gym class and prayed to God none of the boys would find me playing Kitty Club with the girls during lunch.

I decided to prepare for the upcoming New York City Marathon in the hopes that I would be able to enter the race by a stroke of good fortune. By this time, I was running at least thirteen miles a day to escape the fact that indeed I was a homosexual without health insurance, any credible source of stable income, and spreading myself thin, both physically and follicularly. Running, much like performing, was exposing my deep need for validation, and to avoid a world that honestly scared me.

I noticed my stamina increase over the months and on two auspicious occasions the security guard at Riverbank Park spoke over the loudspeaker in a bold and commanding voice, "You there! Please stop running! The park has been closed for over an hour and you are trespassing." I noticed there hadn't been anyone on the track for an awfully long time and the lights had consequently been turned off. So, slightly embarrassed but pumped full of endorphins, I finished my lap, ran up the hill to the 143rd street exit, jumped the fence and ran back to my apartment for a hot shower before hitting the hay.

I tried to think of ways I could enter the race. Stalking a famous runner and getting arrested was completely out of the question, since authority figures appealed to my need for structure, and I wasn't all that interested in finding my first real boyfriend in prison. So, I continued to run every day and work at a restaurant at night, scheming and dreaming of Epsom salt bubble baths and dry-rubbed, free-range, chicken au jus.

Then came a certain smell rising from my feet like an invisible smoke signal. I used to attribute my body's natural inability to smell bad to good genes, but after finding my father's socks in the dirty laundry and being able to pinpoint the exact location of my mother's work shoes while on the opposite side of the house, I realized no one can go through life always smelling like roses.

My hygienic ritual was consistent even though I had been known to forget to clip my toenails on more occasions than I care to mention. I may very well have punctured unsuspecting victims along their backsides, legs, and face amidst the heat of unbridled passion. I'd even ripped gaping holes in cotton socks and lightweight pants by my oversight in fastidious grooming. Still, I'd always prided myself on meticulousness when it came to overall personal cleanliness.

Yet ever since taking up running, I simply couldn't wait to come home after a hard day's work and rub a sharp object vigorously along the soles of my feet for irritatingly long increments of time. Startled downstairs neighbors would jump from their reclining Lazy-Boys at the sound of my bed creaking back and forth with a moderate consistency of tempo and fury. Heavy breathing suppressed by moaning and light panting, mixed with psychotic bouts of laughter through grit teeth in the presence of physical titillation and egregious childlike pleasure, would cause anyone in earshot to arouse suspicion and curiosity.

Even Stella, my roommate's dog, wouldn't go near my feet. Yet she would shit on the bathroom rug and gobble it up like a hotdog before I got a chance to scold her with an extended pointer finger. I wonder if it was Athlete's Foot, or a very interesting way of my body telling me to stop moisturizing areas that were not properly aerated or exposed to direct sunlight. If that was what being an "athlete" entailed, then I'd have been happier prancing around on marley and getting floor burns in dance class. The soreness and muscular fatigue of unnatural body movements I could handle, but the permanent cloud of foot odor that followed me like a shadow of doubt, or a red mark on my permanent record in high school, was just too much for me to handle in mixed company.

The only way I got through my long runs without blisters or chaffed nipples was a heavy dose of Vaseline strategically placed on high traction areas of skin under high-tech, waterproof, and flame-retardant running apparel. I thought that one day I was going to run a marathon and finally be able to say I did something instead of waiting around for another opportunity to pass me by. I guess the pain and agony of this process was a small price to pay for eminent glory and the personal satisfaction of a job well done.

As any stroke of luck would have it, the real story began when I went to see an acquaintance of mine in a horrific showing of *Taming of the Shrew* at the 42nd Street Studio Theatre. It was a Friday night, and I was totally alone, per usual, with nothing better to do to start my weekend off with a bang than sit and watch a re-run of *Grey's Anatomy* with a box of reduced-fat Cheez-Its in my lap. I had been happy to at least get out of the apartment for a while.

It was one of those workshops that never receive enough funding and are only produced by people either for the love of their craft or for something more artistic to prove. Of course, when my friend came out of the dressing room after the show I had only positive comments to make. “Those buttons on Kate's dress were fabulous and that Petruccio, I couldn’t believe he never stumbled on a line.”

During intermission, I saw a woman with a yellow ING-Marathon jacket on and decided to strike up a conversation to pass the ten minutes we still had left to enjoy our freedom. I asked her if she was racing next week. She smiled widely, and chuckled as she said, "Good Heavens, no! No, I work for the Marathon. I don't run unless I have to catch a bus." I smiled even wider trying to imagine her doing so. I remarked about how exciting it must be to work for such a prestigious event, and that I longed to take part in the race but had not known I needed to qualify before the deadline months earlier.

Her mood changed abruptly, and her demeanor became encouraging. "Oh, you still can! We need guides." I shook my head slowly from side to side and furrowed my brow in an attempt at recalling what I had read on the website about qualifications and processing fees.

"I...don't know what you mean," I stammered. She paused a little longer and smiled again, only this time she looked like the Fairy Godmother, seconds from tapping me on the forehead with her magic wand making all my wildest dreams come true.

She got closer, nudged me, and whispered, "Come to the Javit's Center next week. We are signing up volunteers to run as guides for handicapped athletes. You must register by this Thursday, or you'll miss your chance. Ask for Achilles."

She gripped the handrails and hobbled up the stairs that led to the vending machines as I scampered off toward the bathroom to check what was left of my hair. With my eyes scanning the wall behind her head I mentally wrote down what she had said and thanked her for the information. *Who the hell was Achilles,* I thought to myself as we went our separate ways, and *why was she whispering this information to me like we were in a spy movie?*

Throughout the entire second act, I became exponentially more excited about helping with the race. I tried to figure out how I was going to get to the Javit's Center by Thursday. I was on such a high from all of the social activism work I was currently involved in and felt that assisting a handicapped athlete in a marathon would be an even greater opportunity for me to feel better about my failed lot in life. I was going to have the chance to run in the greatest race in the world! The wheels began to turn. I had to do this, and time was ticking away at an alarming rate.

The show ended with a horrendous Brechtian monologue by Kate disturbing the dinner solemnly rising in my esophagus. I left the theatre in the middle of a torrential downpour looking for the uptown A train, praying to God that it was still running express to save what little patience I had left.

That week ticked by and all I thought about was the looming race. I was finding it more and more difficult to quell an aching desire to gouge out my eyes every painstaking hour of rehearsal each night. I had hoped things would have gotten better after spending a month and a half with the company. I was dying rather slowly on the inside from the entire process. With its costly expense of my energy and having to take time off of actual paid work, I could not get thoughts of mass murder or ultimate suicide out of my head.

I realized I'd rather be in Hell than choreographically mime my own failed escape out of an aquarium that was rapidly filling with invisible lava. Experimental dance theatre just was not for me. After coming to that conclusion and witnessing the "Music Director" barking like a dog and imitating the sound of a seagull in flight about to hit the side of an oncoming airplane, I quietly picked my bags in protest, had a brief, but professional discussion with the director in the hallway and mimed "Goodbye" to the rest of the cast with a side-to-side motion of my jazz hand and a menacing scowl.

I came to fully appreciate how important it was never to agree to something that can't be explained in logical terms during the proposal period. "Oh, you'll love it! We're doing this thing with birds, and like we're gonna be birds, and there's like wind and stuff and puppets and oh…it's totally cool. You're gonna love it! You'll see."

"No way, Jose! I'm gonna need sketches, blueprints and an iron-clad contract to sign…in triplicate."

I left the rehearsal space at LaMama and walked toward Broadway-Lafayette to catch the uptown D-train. It was the only time in a month and a half that I caught it running express at that stop. For some reason, I could feel that something exciting was happening all around me and it wasn't just the straight couple locking tongues beside me on the platform. This feeling was set into motion the moment I left rehearsal and was epitomized by a rapidly approaching train of subway cars in the distance. I got on, the doors closed with a "Bee, Bong" and I instantly felt better about being a total quitter.

I had to get off work by 6 p.m. the next evening to make it to the Javit's Center by 6:30. I only knew the rough vicinity of where the building could possibly be located, which was on the other side of the island from work. I made it there with about ten minutes to spare.

I rubbed my eyes upon entering the building, and when the trippy blood vessels faded from view, I was immediately swept up in a massive frenzy of activity. There were so many people running around everywhere; the lights and the echoing sounds of buzzing patrons and shoppers were overwhelming my senses. I found someone with a yellow uniform and began asking him where I was. Drifting off from conversation, I saw a sign marked "Achilles" and ran toward the booth. I couldn't wait to meet this guy and tell him the whole story.

An older gentleman at the front pointed me in the direction of registration. He told me to hurry and that they were closing soon. People in the building were obviously under the influence of some highly competitive chemicals. I didn't know if it was because there were only two days left to shop for essentials before the marathon weekend, or that I had unwittingly sucked myself into an energy vortex hidden behind the building's tinted glass after passing through those heavy, giant, metal revolving doors. I could have pulled down my pants and sang *Nessun Dorma* and no one would have noticed, but had I pulled out a yellow armband signed by Lance Armstrong, I would have been beaten senselessly into a pile of mashed potatoes, viciously burglarized, and left for dead on the freshly waxed marble floor.

The young woman at the desk spoke softly. She was completely exhausted from an entire day of volunteer work and protein deficiency. I blamed her lack of energy on the empty bag of potato chips casually dropped in the wastepaper basket beside her, next to a copy of Cosmopolitan and a three-liter plastic bottle of Diet-Coke.

After introductions, she asked me, "What is your projected time?" I looked at the wall clock by the sock sale and told her that it was almost 6:30 p.m., and if we were going to do this thing she'd better hurry up and give me some papers to sign before her rapidly falling glucose levels hit rock bottom. Since she didn't find my attempt at humor, or my aggressive impatience amusing, the idea of me adding a few knock-knock jokes to break the ice was completely out of the question.

She repeated her question and I finally blurted out, "3:10!" I remembered running for three hours once without stopping and heard someone say that 3:10 was a really good time to shoot for in a marathon. The woman's eyes bugged out of their sockets and she hurriedly scrambled around to find papers and a working pen. You'd think I was Arnold Schwarzeneggar looking to donate sperm or Fabio hoping to drop off a few golden locks at an alopecia convention. I suddenly became the poster boy for a miracle vaccine against cancer, rather than just another guy trying to get into a race through the back door.

She kept talking to me about a visually impaired Polish athlete who needed a runner with that time, and how everyone had been looking for someone like me for an entire week to no avail. Her face was stuck in a stack of papers, so I barely caught the entirety of what she was trying to tell me. The only thoughts that kept running through my head were *How fast can blind people run anyway? How do they do it? Will I need to purchase a cane or a seeing-eye-dog to help me prepare for this role of a lifetime? I can't even afford new running shoes and I've been training on sneakers I bought at Kohl's for $24.99. How the hell am I going to…*

"Here we go, Mr. Seda. Can I have you sign right here?" I didn't have time to think of how I was going to get everything done in three days before the big race. I had a once in a lifetime opportunity in sight, and it was my sight that was going to get me there. Not only was I helping someone in need, which sincerely appealed to me, but I was sure he was going to teach me a thing or two about life in the process. I welcomed the opportunity to be of service, so I signed on the dotted line without hesitation.

I called the hotel where the gentleman was staying and left him a voice message. "Hello, Mari…Oh, I think it says, Marios. Mariusz. Umm…Mr. Gallbladder…Golabek, this is Dan Seda. I'll be running with you in Sunday's race. Please call me back at your earliest convenience as we have much to discuss before the week is through. Thank you…I mean Jin-koo-yeh. That means, 'Thanks,' right? Okay…bye."

Then I thought to myself, "What if he doesn't see the red, blinking light on the answering machine in his hotel room? What if he gets a message from the front desk that I called and, in his haste, to retrieve it he trips and falls headfirst into the nightstand bleeding to death alone in a cruel, foreign land? I would not only be responsible for his demise but for ruining my chances at athletic stardom. *No, calm down! Everything will be fine if I just get to the International Friendship Race tomorrow morning.*

It was Thursday and I had two days to figure out what the hell I was doing running a damn marathon without any equipment or prior knowledge of the sport. Where was my subscription to Runner's magazine? Where was my lifetime supply of Vaseline and fashionable running apparel? I'd never owned a real watch let alone a stopwatch. Who the hell runs their first marathon in 3:10 in New York City without years of serious training under their belt, a regimented diet plan, or a serious death wish?

On Friday, I didn't think of anything but the race. I was so excited I could hardly stand it. I started reading a little bit about how runners prepare and what they eat before and after the race, where they poop if they need to poop along the route and what to do if one's legs suddenly fall off. I went back to the Javit's Center and bought new running shoes that I wore everywhere I went.

The person selling me my shoes was a very sweet young Latina who offered me a discount at the checkout line. She took a picture of the shoes I trained in and passed it around to her colleagues at the Foot Locker kiosk because she'd never seen anything that horrible in all her life. Her coworkers looked at me and covered their mouths in horror.

"You trained in those?"

"Yes...?"

"Damn, boo, you got problems!"

After this humiliating experience, I started bulking up on my carbs by eating lots of pasta and protein for good measure. I learned a lot from the people at the convention; one piece of advice was, "never allow anyone to take pictures of your old shoes." The next day, I was going to purchase the rest of my gear, which included socks, insoles, and running shorts.

I received a call that night from a man named Mario who spoke "very small English." If I was going to help him, I'd better start learning Polish in a matter of hours.

"Hello Danuel, dees ees Maaario. I...am...I run. I...you...Saturrday. Eleven...hour...okay?"

"Ummm. Yes. Sure, Mario. I'd be happy to meet with you tomorrow at eleven for the Pre-race run. Where would you like to...?"

He started to laugh uncomfortably, and I realized he hadn't understood a single word I had just said. So, I decided to just listen and say "Okay" after every exhale and what appeared to be a complete thought.

"No. You speak small English. I no...I big runner...small English...you know?"

"Yes. Okay, Mario."

"Okay. Tomor...tomorrow...you...me...run...eleven... hour...okay?"

"Okay."

"Okay. Tank you Dan, my Amedican friend."

"Okay, Mario. Thank you!"

After hanging up, I had to take a moment to recover from what just transpired. I had no one to tell that this brief conversation that took over fourteen of my precious cellphone minutes and the only information I got from him was to be ready to run on Saturday at 11:00 a.m. Luckily, he was staying at the Chelsea Savoy and I remembered passing it on the 23rd street bus on my way to a debauched gymnastics class at Chelsea Piers. I read a little more of the runner's paperwork before bed and found out all the information I needed to know for the next day. I slept soundly that evening dreaming of pasta and Polka.

On Saturday, I arrived at our designated meeting place in front of the United Nations building. I was mesmerized at the sight before my very eyes. Here was this unbelievable gathering of so many different nations coming together to accomplish one goal and I was the only American for blocks. Much of the city had been marked off with barricades, while police cars and fire trucks directed us safely from the East side up through Central Park West. It was an incredible sight to see!

No one spoke fluent English and the police officers didn't know how to help me find a visually impaired Polish guy named Mario. Honestly, they had more important things to worry about. I asked a few people what the Polish flag looked like just in case he was standing below it with a checkered farm suit and pigtails waiting happily for my arrival. In my haste, I had forgotten to research Polish culture but remembered a few phrases my best friend Chris taught me back in high school. I just wasn't allowed to say a lot of them in sober company.

I finally found a group of short, red-faced individuals huddled in a mass of corrective eyewear keeping warm and stretching wearing red and white matching tracksuits. I introduced myself as the Achilles guide and one of the men took me forcefully by the shoulder and started yelling, "Mario!" He told me to "Stay put!" in harsh-broken English, and he went to find where his comrade had gone to look for me. Eventually, Mario made his way back to the group and we were so excited to finally meet each other face to face.

He was a tall, skinny man with thick glasses that rested on his large bulbous nose behind his oversized ears. His teeth were crooked and yellow but that never stopped him from smiling. His face was covered in acne scars and exuded a gentle, airy spirit. He pulled me around from group to group forcing me to take pictures with all the other nations, holding a Polish flag in one hand and hugging me very tightly with the other. The whole experience was very surreal and even though he was yanking me through hordes of foreigners and making me take pictures with the entire world, you could tell he was truly having the time of his life.

It was incredible! All the love I was being willfully dragged into went against everything I was taught to accept as a New Yorker. It was better than the Vicodin I was prescribed after getting my wisdom teeth extracted, better than my first lover's wondering pointer finger, and better than…well it was pretty high up there on the "Pretty Cool Shit" list. One could easily have fallen in love with the energy surrounding us all. If that was at all any indication of what Europeans were like, then I should be so lucky to spend the rest of my life living abroad and die in Poland.

I only wished someone told us what to wear. I looked around and everyone had on those tight, black running pants to keep their legs warm in the cold, rainy weather. Some even wore those little running shorts to show off their well-defined calves and bulging quadriceps. I had on an old pair of light grey sweatpants and just told everyone that I left my cool clothes at home. I didn't want to show how completely ill-prepared I was to race.

I wore my thin, black zip-up jacket over the stained thermal t-shirt I wore as a soldier in the Columbus Day Parade a month earlier. Thankfully, it was so cold that no one really cared about anything but staying warm. So, I didn't have to worry about being exposed as the poor amateur runner that I was. I just sucked it all up and began the pre-race with a horde of pumped-up internationalists surrounding me in an intoxicatingly comfortable bubble of serotonin and pheromones.

It was the only time since the parade that the streets were empty and devoid of traffic. The city was serene and quiet. It was a crisp, November morning, and the on-lookers cheered for us from their office windows as we joined together in what was to be an eventful weekend for everyone.

That afternoon I went back to the Javit's Center and bought proper clothes. Most of it was on sale because the smart runners had already purchased what they needed days before, but I reveled in buying items at drastically reduced prices, much like my mother whose spending habits rivaled those of Mother Theresa. I bought burgundy running shorts with a zipper pocket in the back and a hidden mesh pocket on the inside at the front, as well as high-tech socks and insoles that were perfectly matched to meet the physiological needs of my lower appendages. Undoubtedly, I looked as though I had been transformed into the Bionic Man. I was given a free running shirt when I signed up and couldn't wait to go home and try on all my new clothes for Stella.

That night before the race we had a pasta party. That's where all the runners gorge themselves on carbohydrates, so they don't die the day of the marathon. I met with Mario and we mimed a great deal of our conversation over the booming dance-party music and overzealous hosts. Coors was one of the many sponsors that night whose lovely promotional models offered us all free cans of beer upon entry into the heated tents at Tavern on the Green. *What moron wants to get drunk the night before a long ass run?* Looking ahead toward the dining room, the Germans and the Irish were having a grand ol' time. Other than that, the food was practically tasteless but there was lots of it, so I helped myself to seconds knowing full well it might be my last meal ever.

Mario and I got closer over dinner. We discussed our lives and our fondness for kielbasa. We found commonalities and distinct differences that made our bond that much closer as new friends. He looked right at me and said, "Daan, if problem tomorrow…I run big…you run big…no problem, okay?" I tried to understand what he meant and asked him to clarify a bit further. He used the same words but different hand gestures and even larger facial expressions in case I might have missed them the first time.

What I got from our intimate moment together was that if anything happened during the race, he would be fine running by himself. I looked at him affectionately and said, "I protect you…I help you." He didn't get it at first. So, I repeated myself only using the International sign for "hug" and "love" while making a cute, puppy-dog face. He eventually backed off a little and laughed it off uncomfortably. I think he got the idea but was just afraid I was asking him for a reach-around. I felt it was my job to see to it that he finished the race safely and on his time. I already knew I would finish somehow. The question now was *how* and *when*?

Upon leaving the party, we got free boxes of wheat pasta and an apple from the nice ladies behind the white, plastic fold-out tables and were escorted outside into the cold city night. Before we left, I took Mario's arm and guided him down the stairs. He didn't understand why I was being so helpful. I just didn't want him to break his leg. I had extensive stake in his ability to remain mobile. He was clearly a functioning member of society who just so happened to have a heavy prescription for corrective eyewear.

We made it down the stairs of the tavern and he told me again, "Daan. Thank you, my friend. I tomorrow run, you run, if problem…anytime, you run, I run, no problem." I looked at his face and there was a definite sign of anxiety behind his eyes, as if he knew I was a well-meaning fraud.

I didn't understand why I was even there to help him. He ran the Luxembourg marathon solo two weeks prior without a guide. He obviously didn't need me and it all just seemed liked an unnecessary logistical procedure. I guess he wasn't scared so much as hoping things would work out for the both of us. He trained very hard for this race and didn't want the same thing to happen that occurred the year prior. He was late to the starting line because he missed his bus. He had mentioned this debacle between mouthfuls of pasta primavera and linguini with clam sauce.

That moment at the steps outside Tavern on the Green was all I thought about the entire night before drifting off to sleep. I set my alarm and dozed off knowing how important tomorrow was for so many reasons.

Sunday, the day of the race, I woke up at 4:30 a.m. to meet Mario at his hotel by 5:40 a.m. All I had to do was take a five-minute shower and put on the clothes I laid out for myself the night before with carbohydrate gel packets stuffed into the pockets, securely zipped, and grab my bag of essential sundries that was still leaning against my bedroom door. I was out of my apartment in Harlem by 4:45 a.m., right on time, and at the subway station by 4:50 a.m. I had an hour to kill so nothing could go wrong.

After not hearing a single train for fifteen minutes, I asked around to see what the problem was. The train I thought was running on time had alterations to its regular schedule conveniently accommodating for the day's marathon festivities. I had no way of knowing what the hell to do. I wanted to rip my face off and douse myself in kerosene.

The train came a half an hour later, slowly sauntering into the station like a lazy lapdog. By this time, I was pissing my short shorts. Not only had I not woken up this early in almost a decade, but on the most important day of my life the train was late and there was a homeless man sitting next to me using a newspaper to dry his underarms after a much-needed spit bath.

I tried everything in my power to remain calm and think of things I could do to get downtown sooner. I had no money for a cab. I had no cell phone to call the hotel. I came with every essential I had to throw it all away when I got to the starting line. Thirty-seven thousand people and there's gotta be at least a few hundred kleptomaniacs among the bunch. You just can't be too careful in New York City.

It was 5:15 a.m. when my connecting train screeched into the station. Every second I sat in my seat, I was trying to telepathically communicate to the conductor, "For the love of God…Step on it! Would ya?" I saw a handful of other runners getting on the local 1-train at different stops along the way. It was amazing to see the differences among people you'd never expect to run marathons: young professionals in shorts and corporate executives with their hair held back with scrunchies and headbands. One prevailing aspect was that they all had a unique glow about them that couldn't be denied. It was the glow of determination with a dose of manic compulsion.

The 1-train didn't go any lower than Times Square 42nd street, so when the doors opened, I bolted up the steps to get onto the street level as if every step was a long-jump hurdle. Without any warm-up, I sprinted down Broadway to the Chelsea Savoy that was twenty blocks away. I got there at 5:45am on the dot. Out of breath, I asked the concierge, "I need to speak to Mario Golabeck in room..." *Oh my God, I forgot the little piece of paper that Mario had written his room number on back at my apartment in the kitchen next to the spice rack! Ummm…okay, don't panic. You're an actor…think on your feet, damn it!*

"Listen, do you have a bunch of Polish people staying at your hotel who are running in the marathon today?" The gentleman behind the desk was not amused and hated the fact that a crazy-looking White kid with a bandana on his head was asking him funny questions.

"No, I'm serious. I need Mario Golabeck in room 1-18…or 1-14, I don't remember." He looked at me with tired eyes and said, "We can't just ring people's room, sir. You'll have to tell me what room he is in." Frustrated, I yelled, "Look him up in your damn book or the fucking computer or something. I'm running in the Goddamn New York City Marathon today and I'm late for the bus! Now, cut the shit and find Golabeck. G-O-L…"

"Okay sir, calm down. He's in room 118."

I could hear every pulsating ring from the receiver in his hands and it made me think how five minutes could have destroyed my chances of helping someone in need run the most important race of *my* life. I was devastated. I waited for what seemed an eternity.

"No one's picking up, sir. Maybe I could..." I was already in the elevator and the doors were closing, as he looked up from the reservation book to finish his last sentence. I didn't care. I let down an entire country of visually impaired Polish people and it was all my fault.

I knocked confidently on room 118 with no answer. I then walked up and down the hallway yelling "Mario" in as best a Polish accent as possible. It came out a little Russian and I wasn't in the mood to break out my Gillian Lane-Plescia "Accents for Actors" CD at that point in time. Like a mad man, I raced down the fire exit and headed out the door before the cleaning lady knew what hit her.

It was 5:55 a.m. and the last bus was going to leave Manhattan at 6:30 a.m. But where the hell was the bus and where the hell was I? Yes, I was in Chelsea. That was clear by all the rainbow flags and beautifully decorated storefront windows, but I had no clue where the Achilles bus was going to leave from, and it was still dark outside. I was completely terrified.

I asked the few New Yorkers who were awake at that time on a Sunday morning how to catch a bus to Staten Island, but they weren't the type of people who could direct me anywhere above ground. I suddenly remembered reading something about Bryant Park on one of the information sheets I got at the Javits Center. I raced on foot to East Midtown from the Lower West Side and along the way I met a representative from Team Holland. I asked her if I could hitch a ride on her bus and she told me that I had to have been invited to ride with them. I pleaded with her to allow me safe passage aboard her vessel and told her my story in a matter of seconds. I even showed her my bib with the numbers on it and everything. She didn't budge.

So, I told her how ridiculous I thought windmills and tulips were to represent a stupid country like Holland and that wearing wooden shoes in the twenty-first century was simply ludicrous. Then, I proceeded to yodel in her face while giving her my middle finger, as I made a dramatic exit by running across the street like a lunatic. I glanced back to see if she had a sudden epiphany of goodwill, but she stood motionless for a few seconds on the corner of 6th Avenue and 28th street and eventually continued walking west to catch her awaiting bus.

I yelled dramatically, "Curse you, Holland, for you have offended me greatly! Beware the wrath of Dan, for it may very well seize you in the form of a muscle spasm during your most difficult hour!"

I stormed uptown kicking trashcans and dodging puddles of dog piss. While running I thought to myself how stereotypically American I had just behaved in front of--what I'm sure was on any other given day--a nice athlete from a country of nice people. Still, I had other things more important on my mind like helping Poland beat Sweden across the finish line in just over three hours. "I will succeed! Damn it. I will succeed!"

I ran up 6th Avenue and approached 34th street Herald Square when I met a man who was, like me, running late to catch the last bus. Coincidentally, he was an American. We made our way up the avenue and reached the longest line of human beings I've ever witnessed since the American Idol audition of 2005. I got on and scanned every single runner looking for Mario. I yelled his name through the mass like a scorned woman looking for her cheating husband. Not a hint of kielbasa in the bunch. My body completely sunk, as I found my place at the end of the line. I crouched down like a tribesman taking a dump in the dirt, started drinking Gatorade, and eating a banana to make myself feel better about being a total loser.

A woman who radiated a kind of glow from the inside out and whose husband had just gone to the local deli to pick up a newspaper and a fresh cup of coffee came over to me to see what was wrong. She immediately made me feel very comfortable, so I didn't want to burden her with my story of bad luck. I listened to other peoples' conversations around me to try and tune out my grief. Some came from all over the United States to run and others chose to prepare for the race by ingesting a devised regimen of supplements suggested by their primary-care physicians for the past eight months.

One woman's office even threw a party for her that Friday complete with a fat-free strawberry yogurt cake topped with vanilla-flavored carbohydrate gel icing. The very thought made me want to hurl. She was so happy that the idea of regurgitation subsided long enough for me to fake a smile when they glanced down at me sitting on the curb by the gutter like a homeless man on one of those subway advertisements.

I got up and joined the huddled mass of runners creeping their way up two lines in order to get a seat on one of the hundreds of buses taking us all to our shared destination. I could see in the distance where the busses were arriving and departing. I didn't know how I was going to do it, but I was going to get on that bus and find Mario if it was the last thing I did.

I eventually lost track of the coffee lady and was kinda glad to not have to overhear the cake lady talk about her slew of successful knee surgeries. I cut ahead and went down the line asking any of the volunteers if they had seen the Achilles bus, Mario or the Polish team. I was completely out of luck and started feeling like I was rapidly going insane if I wasn't already. The sun was peeking around the side of the Trump building and the line of late runners wrapped around the city for blocks.

Everything I was supposed to be doing wasn't happening and I had no one else to blame but myself. The lines divided into other lines and security guards were standing by just in case anyone went berserk. There was a definite "Survival of the Fittest" quality raging within the people around me and I was afraid I'd have to eat someone to find a place on the bus. Luckily, one of the buses pulled around the corner and a couple of us jumped the line and took a seat near the back. No one protested.

Upon entering the charter bus, I saw a familiar face and sat next to her. She was the coffee woman I had met in line, and we ended up chatting for an hour. I was feeling a little less stressed about things since there was nothing else that I could physically do at the time. So we shared laughs, stories, and a little advice.

I told her what had happened that morning. She told me not to worry and that it would all work out somehow. She taught me about Chi energy and how to use it while running. I told her about my life and overcoming obstacles and she told me about her life in Madison, Wisconsin and how running has been an integral part of her spiritual life. We could see the sun coming up over the bridge leading us into Staten Island where the race was to begin. When we stopped, she told me to get going because I had a job to do. I wished I had thought about getting her information before we parted ways, but I had one thing on my mind and the clock was ticking.

Everyone had green, orange, or blue bibs on and had to report to the field corresponding to their designated color to keep some civility within all the madness. Only half the buses had arrived and already it felt like a Pete Seeger concert at Madison Square Garden. I asked anyone with a walky-talky where the Achilles booth was. *Maybe Mario would find me there?* I would notice his shaved head poking out of the tiny crowd of red and white tracksuits and eyeglasses. He'd find me comatose in a pile of banana peels, drunk off Gatorade martinis, and exhaling protein bar wrappers.

I notified the people at the Achilles booth to be on the lookout for Mario, as I went on foot to search the grounds for him excusing myself for having major trust issues. For hours I was on my feet walking from field to field in search of one man out of thirty-seven thousand people. The odds were completely against me. Eventually, there was nothing I could do but sit and wait, which made the whole ordeal seem completely insurmountable.

The people in the booth decided to give me a different athlete to guide since I was such a horrible human being. He was a paraplegic and had two high-tech running stilts that made him look like a gigantic praying mantis. He took one look at me from above and scoffed. I guess it was my bleach-stained sweatpants, or the fact that my skin-tight t-shirt read "Keepin' It Rural."

He replied to the woman smugly after looking me over a few times, "If zat ees all you can offerr zen zat vill haf to do, but only if zat zer ees zee only opshun."

I was shocked! I was appalled. I was seconds from queening him off his stilts. They gave me a new colored bib with a different set of numbers on it. They pinned Gruyere's number on top of Mariusz's, as I stared eye-level to the French guy's knee skis and growled. I thanked the woman like any good Southern boy would and told the enemy I'd meet him at the starting gate. He didn't want my help and obviously he didn't need it. I wanted Mario back and fast! I couldn't just sit back and not look for him one last time.

It was now thirty minutes until the start of the race, and I was in an unbelievably difficult situation. *What to do*? *Do I run the marathon and try to catch up with Mario who would most assuredly be running much faster than I? How would I even hope to find him in all the chaos?* We never got far enough in our translations from Polish hand gestures to spoken English to even consider universally understood mating calls. I had to decide, and it had to be a good decision. I could feel a surge of tears and rage building up inside me. I left my bag of banana peels and empty protein bar wrappers on the walk path next to the overfilled trashcans and ran to the entrance.

There were so many people already lined up down the street. The line stretched for miles, and I saw signs up above people's heads stating their projected finish times. "4:30, 4:20, 4:10…3:50, 3:40." I snaked my way through the entire crowd of literally thousands of people. I still had my sweat-clothes on over my running gear to keep me warm and ready at a moment's notice to tear away. I wasn't turning back, not for a second. I got this far, and I was not going to give up.

I got up to the 3:30's when the line began to move toward the starting gate. I knew that Mario was far ahead in the distance where the 3:10's were positioned, yet I just could not make it there in time. It was literally impossible. I remembered what he said at the pasta dinner about if something happened to either of us that we should run the race solo and know that we were still a team no matter what. Or at least that's what I understood in Gay.

I quickly tore off my top clothes and gloves, joining the line like a wounded soldier ready for my final battle. There was an overwhelming sense of excitement and anticipation in the air that seemed to center my anxiety. The line stopped moving once we curved around the parking lot and I could see in the distance the bridge that was to be our first hurdle.

I heard two gentlemen behind me discussing their options of payback if one beat the other to the finish line. One gentleman contested, "I just wanna make it to the end, dude." I thought that was cute and it instantly made me smile, because it was exactly how I felt. People began throwing off layers of clothing and hurling them into the air like caps at a graduation ceremony. They landed on the roofs of the parked buses with soft thuds that the more rambunctious athletes were capriciously jumping from. The excitement was remarkably palpable.

A man on the loudspeaker was getting us all pumped up, as the cast from *Jersey Boys* sang the "National Anthem." Not a singer around me, yet everyone thought themselves to be Pavarottis, especially the Russians. A line of back hair and balding heads stretched as far as the eye could see. The gun was fired! It took a while for the trickle effect to hit each wave of times runners.

Within a matter of seconds, I brought my knees up to my chest to pop my hips, touched the ground with the palms of my hands to stretch out my hamstrings in a space not unlike a crowded subway car. I twisted my spine to get out any loose ends, being careful not to hit anyone around me. I cracked my neck a few times and shook my shoulders up and down to get out any remaining tension.

I tore off the red Achilles t-shirt I had on over my running apparel to keep me warm, as I was now running the marathon alone and could not, in good conscience, be identified as an Achilles guide without my partner. I took off my top bib and pinned Mario's number back onto my chest in his honor. There wasn't a doubt in my mind whether I was going to finish the race; it was merely a question of when.

I was moments from starting a twenty-six-point two mile run through New York City and its surrounding boroughs in one of the most prestigious marathons in the world, without properly stretching, training, or having any of the experience most of the runners I'd be next to possessed. Most importantly, I was without my dear friend, Mario.

There were so many emotions and thoughts running through my mind that I hardly knew what to make of it all. I barely had time to catch my breath and look down to see if my shoelaces were tied when we were off and running.

Adventures of a Young, Social Activist

Being an openly gay East Coaster, I learned most of what I knew about Kansas from a movie involving red sparkly shoes and the repetitive mantra, "There's no place like home!" After all, what man with an "artistic temperament" and a penchant for aromatherapy candles wouldn't love the idea that somewhere over the rainbow lies a magical land filled with opportunities to make a difference in someone's life? I was upset to find out that there were hardly any wicked witches in Kansas and that these sightings were only reported to have occurred on Halloween.

On tour, I did find the majority of Kansonians to be gracious, hospitable people, willing to go out of their way to help you find a bottle of Mucinex at the local drugstore and point you in the general direction of a Golden Corral restaurant for lunch. What was even more surprising was our unequivocal welcome onto the campus of MidAmerica Nazarene University. Never had we, as Equality Riders, been granted this kind of respect and overwhelming encouragement on our journey across America.

We were met outside the dining hall by faculty and administration with genuine smiles and outstretched palms. We were given breakfast and met with our host for the day. My host was Paul, a computer science major and an all-around great guy. We talked about faith, love, computers, and about our common interests in teaching children.

My presentation group was on at 9am and we made our way to Mr. Haye's class after breakfast to present *In God's Image: A Look at Love in Scripture.* I was floored to see rows of attentive open eyes and ears that early in the morning. Students and faculty were frantically writing down information and questions to ask us. When it was all over the students shook our hands and we ended in a prayer of solidarity. There was interaction, involvement, and wholesome dialog that lasted well after the class ended. Not many of our stops on tour were like this, which is why it sticks out in my mind so vividly.

Paul introduced me to countless students and there was a felt sense that who we were as human beings was accepted upon meeting us. It was as if there was a clean slate, a chance to be seen as human for the first time in a long time. There was a real sense that our differences were not as dramatic as one might assume and that everyone in the room, no matter their sexual orientation or identity, simply desired love and acceptance.

At 11 a.m., I went with Paul to hear a presentation of *International Perspectives on LGBT issues.* I can say with all honesty that I learned more about my people and my community at large than I ever thought possible. Who would have known that diversity within our group could continue to amaze me even during the times we shared our most intimate moments: our joys and our fears, our bad hair days, and morning breath?

At 12 p.m., we had lunch and I met even more of Paul's friends. I didn't feel like I was on show or forced to answer outlandish questions like I had at other schools. I was treated as a guest, but more importantly, as a human being. I observed, listened, reflected, conversed, ate, laughed, sang, and made new friends. I learned what a Granger cookie was and that every school has its unwavering opinion regarding the inappropriateness of wearing sweaters sporting the names of rival schools on campus. Apparently, it's a big no-no in the Midwest, wherever you go.

Lunch ended and the Equality Riders made their way into a smaller room with beautiful chandeliers and round tables. We discussed with the minister ways in which the school could improve their policies of inclusion. I felt strongly that the impact of our visit left a huge impression, not only on the administrators, faculty, and students, but on us as riders too. I don't think we smiled that much in a long time.

Yes, we understood our work was important and we knew that there was a fine line between what we did as activists and how we interacted when the pressure wasn't directly on us. But our visit had been so perfect the entire day that we felt an obligation to hold on to our collective happiness for as long as we could; that way it would make our next stop at Brigham Young University that much more tolerable and our call to action that much more evident.

We walked outside with a blast of cold air on our faces toward the big, gay bus. Everyone circled up, took pictures, said our goodbyes, and we ended with a prayer of solidarity. It was too perfect, and I was just waiting for Fred Phelps to come along with one of his famous signs reading "God Hates Fags!" Thankfully, that never happened, although he and his followers did threaten to do so several times.

All in all, I realized that assumptions might be the root of all evil. The only way to fully live is to learn to love in a way that includes rather than excludes. It's awfully difficult to learn this important idea if we do not have the means to educate ourselves properly by getting out there and meeting the world with open arms and an open heart. Perhaps, the ride offered me much more than a two-month chance to make a difference in the world. Maybe the biggest change was within me. I thought I'd hold on to Kansas for just a little while longer.

I missed a lot of normal life while traveling the country on a big, gay bus. It was the comfortable clichés of a humdrum life that I craved between pee breaks and trips to convenience stores. Perhaps, because we were all so similar, yet so incredibly varied in our personal interests, that our common ties were becoming overshadowed by individual annoying quirks.

I peered out the one-way window at each passing tree as another mile was clocked off our fearless bus driver, Travis's, speedometer. With my legs fully stretched out, resting on the seat in front of me, I questioned where my life was headed, where it had been, and where I was in all the seemingly chaotic silence of life on the road.

Each rumble of the engine and bump in the road was a constant reminder of our collective reality. Yet, when we stood hand in hand, arm in arm, singing spirituals on the front line at another unwelcoming university, I was reminded of the joyous times. Those moments were unforgettable, like when we stood together on a sunny peak overlooking the Pacific Ocean, or when we hiked up the tallest crest in Provo, Utah, at sunset watching the sky change colors. I wondered if what we were doing was really happening or if it was all just a dream.

My friends and family were now the twenty-five other riders sleeping, listening to music, and reading the Bible, Dean Koontz, and Anne Rice beside me on the big, gay bus we called home. I knew them intimately: the funny ways they fell asleep, their likes and dislikes, how they handled stress and tackled hard issues like politics, religion, and homosexuality. It was the closest thing I'd had to camaraderie in a very long time.

My trip across the country showed me things I would never have seen in a million years. Even if I had all the money in the world, it would be impossible to come close to all that I had witnessed with my own senses. Granted we didn't get to see the Grand Canyon that trip, but we did spend an hour in the redwood forest in California. I spent most of my time there doing yoga on a picnic table, exposing the new tattoo I got in San Francisco the week before to the sun. We picked eucalyptus leaves and sucked the juices out of their creases. We thought that would cure the sinus infections that were ravaging everyone on the bus at the time.

I saw a lot of purple buds on bushes by the highway. There were reflections of mountains, evergreen trees, and little, tiny patches of sky that were scattered about the calm waters of Northern California's vast and distant lakes like lily pads in a Monet painting. From the bus window everything looked small enough to eat, climb onto with our fingertips, or squash with our thumbnails. Maybe one day I'd find that kind of peace when I could finally sit down and stop fighting the daemons I'd been wrestling with.

There had been times in my life where writing seemed the only plausible, healthy escape. I would also run my problems away instead of losing myself in a bottle, which could be seen as a good thing. That way I could sweat out the issues I had before needing the time to really think about them. Still, even when I ran, I found other things to worry about. I guess there's no real way of escaping your problems because you usually find your way back to them waiting for you to be acknowledged and dealt with.

I sat in a lonely hotel room in Rexburg, Idaho, wishing I were home, but not for obvious reasons. Home, at least for me, meant something other than the cookies and milk images you see in Rembrandt's and in Coca Cola commercials. Every year I grew a little older and a little balder, I realized that your home is what you make of it. Nothing is ever "perfect." It just is what it is and if something's not working you try to fix it. If you can't fix it, then you might have a bigger problem on your hands. The people who will love you the most are those you consider your family--whether biological or not--and that's really all that matters.

I just needed to get away from it all. Being a dancer, I knew that when things got tough and all you wanted to do was fall right there on the stage, there was something that kicked in inside you when you needed it most. It was an indescribable feeling that surpassed logic, and I knew it was dormant inside me, just waiting for the opportunity to jumpstart my heart. But at that point in my life, I couldn't find my heart at all.

I was embarrassed to say it, but I was at a loss that was too painful to deny. I was mentally tired, emotionally exhausted, and was sick and unsure of everything in my life. I had been crying all the time where no one could see it. Something had to give. I knew I had to leave the tour, but I just didn't know where to go. Maybe it was how I was raised--essentially being thrown to the wolves--or it could have been pride or the learning opportunities inherent in the challenges with struggle. Whatever the case was, I was not happy and didn't know what happiness even looked like anymore.

After we left California, we traveled north to Portland, Oregon. We stayed in our first nice hotel and had a rare opportunity to spend the day by ourselves to enjoy the city. I had been so depressed for weeks and the loneliness had gotten to me. That night, I ventured out to a dance club with a few of the other riders and for the first time in a long time I let loose like there was no tomorrow. I met an attractive young man there who made me feel desired. Drunk, and not caring about myself, we took a taxi to his house to spend the night. Wanting to end it all, but also to feel something one last time, I undressed and met him in the shower.

He kept assuring me that I had nothing to worry about and that he would never lie to someone as beautiful as me. He kept telling me that I was, "So hot!" In a moment of vulnerability, he entered my body without me having time to react. I looked at him dead in the eyes, but it was too late. I told him to stop and put a condom on like I had asked him before. This time, he agreed. I came with the backs of my knees caressing his biceps and with my back pressed firmly into the indentation of the bathroom sink.

I was in Rexburg, Idaho, and we were preparing to launch a demonstration at Brigham Young University's campus when I received a call from the doctor. I couldn't blink my eyes the entire time and I hung up the phone after calling in my prescription to the local pharmacy with my voice noticeably shaking.

I slammed my fist into the pillow that I carried all the way from Raleigh. It had been a present from Lindsay to help me sleep at night. I'd always had trouble sleeping through the night, as far back as I could remember. Perhaps, it was the fact that I was left home alone most night and would be woken up by my older brother and his friends beating the door down for late-night binges when my mother was at work. It could have been the fact that I was petrified aliens were going to come and abduct me that I had to crawl in my little brother's bed, making sure not to wake him up, because I had no one there to protect me. I was a truly tortured kid and bore way too much responsibility that deeply affected me and my poor decisions later in life.

I beat the wooden headboard of my bed in yet another shitty motel room for several minutes so hard that I went deaf and couldn't hear the cheap, springed mattress creak any longer. I was sweaty and my eyes wouldn't close. I buried myself in the bed and couldn't speak for hours. I don't know why I didn't just end it all right there and then.

I asked a fellow rider to go with me to the pharmacy in this little Mormon town in the middle of nowhere. The pharmacist took one look at me with my grey Soulforce jacket on and angrily handed me my medicine. We were already regional celebrities and jokingly referred to as "those faggots on the big, gay bus." We left and never returned.

That night Alexey slept by my side and brushed my forehead with his hand. He was one of the co-directors on the bus and my major confidant while on the ride. He cried a few times when he thought I was asleep. I heard him but couldn't open my eyes because I knew that he would feel embarrassed if he knew that I saw him. He loved me as did everyone on the ride. I wonder why it was so difficult for me to love myself.

At four in the morning, I left Rexburg and the Equality Ride for good. A broken-down car with a painted sign on the door that read "Airport Shuttle" pulled into the parking lot of our motel in the bleak, drizzling rain. I gathered the letters the other riders wrote to me in the night and put them in my pockets that were stuffed with Kleenex. Haven and Alexey were outside under an umbrella to make sure I was safe, and I looked around at part of the country I thought I would never have seen.

There were a few familiar faces in the windows holding their hands up to the cold frosty glass to wave goodbye. I got into the car and headed to the closest airport, which was about three hours away. The rain poured down in droves so much that the windshield wipers on the taxi stopped working and we had to pull off the road to wait out the storm. Inside, I felt a hollow emptiness. Without the capacity to feel, I used the rain as my excuse to keep from crying.

Once I got to Raleigh, I quickly admitted myself into a mental hospital for evaluation and treatment. It was clear that I needed help and so I took the first steps toward claiming back my life. I was diagnosed with depression and given several coping strategies that would help me adjust to life on anti-depressants. I also met a woman around my age named Victoria, who would become a dear friend and my saving grace.

There was a young girl whose mother had just dropped her off to be admitted into inpatient care. It was as if she was being abandoned, and there was this vacant, lost look behind her eyes. I remembered those feelings from childhood. It took a while for her to break out of her shell, but after talking with me for a few minutes I told her that everything was going to be all right. I was also coaxing myself to believe the very same thing, which was another strategy I employed for others growing up. She smiled in a childish way that I cannot fully describe; one that may have been used to appease someone you didn't really care for because they wouldn't fully understand. It was a smile of deep empathy clouded in doubt.

An American Idol re-run was on the television above the check-in window, and I began to lose myself singing Clay Aiken's rendition of *Bridge Over Troubled Water*. A voice from the front desk yelled, "Go head, boy. You betta sang!"

I looked around and noticed the security guard leaning over the counter hollering at me. "You better not let that voice go to waste, son. You singin' in church?" I laughed a little with weary eyes and spoke with her about my life as a performer and activist.

"Oh, well…Catholics ain't got nothin' on Baptists when it comes to praisin' the Lord!"

"Yeah, I suppose you're right," I answered, slightly defeated.

I left her smiling and chatting with the receptionist as I passed the young girl who was now balled up on the couch with a stuffed animal held tightly to her chest. I smiled and watched her as she slowly but deliberately lifted her head and exposed a straight row of shiny, white teeth.

I often felt like I didn't belong there. Especially when I was the one leading the discussions and offering advice during group therapy sessions, which the facilitator was both surprised by and abhorred. She was a miserable, middle-aged woman with a medium-length, silver bob cut with bangs, who hated her job; so, I did everything I could to make sure the patients around me were treated with compassion and dignity. There were also times when I felt right at home, like I was in school learning valuable lessons that I would use later in life.

People have the perception that those who seek help for mental issues are weak. My experiences with these individuals would prove otherwise. In fact, it is up to the individual to pick up the pieces of their broken lives where medicine and intervention fall short. That was often an arduous road, especially when surrounded by people who could never understand.

In all actuality the patients at the hospital were some of the strongest people I'd ever met. I was certain that saner people could not have dealt with half the things I'd heard come out of those people's mouths. They were living, breathing examples of the power of grace, walking the narrow line between sanity and insanity every day of their lives. Often prisoners in their own minds and bodies, their courage and their stories were unquestionably profound. It was impossible for me not to respect them for just existing. What they chose to do with that existence, many times, depended on their willingness to live. These people were intelligent, sensitive, and grossly undervalued in their outside lives. It's a shame that things had to get so out of hand to jumpstart the healing process for us all. On the flip side, things had to happen to make some people ask for help; especially, if you've never been taught how to do so in the first place.

I felt like a child learning how to walk again. I had to sit back and see how to look at the world in a whole new light. I had been intelligent enough to devise my own coping strategies to deal with the mess I'd been given growing up that only covered up the scars that most people were simply unaware of. I had the world on my shoulders in the hopes that it would make me stronger. The result was still up for interpretation.

At that point, I knew that one day I'd be ready to walk again on my own, but before then it was a slow and steady, step-by-step process. I somehow knew that everything was going to be okay, and if the sun was shining and the birds were chirping, it was a good day to be alive.

A Contemplative Walk

The only sounds I could hear were that of my own rambling thoughts, the "clip-clop" of my sandals, and the scratches they made against the paved walkway. I had taken some time out of the day to be alone with my spirit, to ask a lot of questions, and to be as open as possible to notice the answers. When back home in Raleigh, Shelly Lake had often been my refuge a storm. I thought this was the appropriate setting for a much-needed contemplative walk.

I wasn't properly dressed for such a trek along the winding pathways of water, wood, and pine. I wanted to walk off a great deal more than just water weight in the blistering sun. I had on a tight orange t-shirt with the short sleeves pulled up over my shoulders and a pair of khaki shorts that were both too long and too loose in the waste. I had no belt to hold them up or socks to protect my feet; only a trusty pair of sandals that were in desperate need of some Shoe Goo.

I thought about many things that needed answers like what I was doing, where I'd been, what I wanted my future to look like, and so on. I asked for guidance from God and my angels, for love, answers, strength, and for peace of mind. I breathed in and out, low and deep, and my heart skipped a beat, but eventually found its rhythm again along with my pulse. I wiped sweat from my brow and around the sides of my temples.

I looked down at the wood planks in front of me when other walkers passed by. It was a natural maneuver I learned while living in New York City that I had noticed was becoming an all-to-familiar habit. I smiled and spoke a few casual phrases to those I wished to converse with such as moms with happy kids and seniors out for an afternoon stroll.

I was coming around to the middle of my second mile when I noticed a bird. Its intriguing characteristics defied description, but I would say that its puffed feathers and orange Mohawk were indications of its sheer uniqueness.

It perched itself on a "10 mph" sign. As I admired its beauty, a big, green bug landed directly on the middle of my left bicep. I tried to flick it off, but the only thing that worked to kill it was a quick, hard slap. That slap ended the poor bug's life and its fragmented remains lay scattered all along the inside bend of my arm. All I could say was "Gross!" and use my shirt to wipe off what was left of the carcass.

Just then, a third event caught my attention. It was a loud roar of thunder in the distance. I rounded the bend of my third mile and stopped by a clearing that seemed promising. I knelt for a few moments and gazed longingly at the expansive lake that lay calm and tranquil before me. The horizon and the sky that reflected from the glistening waters were majestic. I thought about how my New York friends would always laugh at me for taking pictures of skies on my outdated cell phone. That was the only way I could stay sane in a city devoid of any sustained level of nature.

I came around the corner and caught a glimpse of a handsome, young Latin man riding his bicycle. I looked down again out of habit and continued to walk forward, but I could feel him staring at me and slowing his pace. As I passed him, he made some sort of sound that caught my attention. I looked back and he was riding very slowly while staring at me.

I thought, that if this was a way of getting my attention that it was ridiculous and so I continued walking toward the bridge nearing the end of my mile. I spotted geese, ducks, and a few swans, and stopped to admire their beauty. Just then, the young man approached me with the bravado of a healthy, young Latin man. The sound of his gears clinking and his tires slowly thumping over the wooden planks of the bridge grew louder and stronger.

He asked me if I lived around the lake. I responded, "No." He said that his name was Quiñonez. I told him that my name was "Dan," knowing full well what the gentleman was getting at.

I watched the water ripple with the wind. He came closer, as if to pounce on his prey, and I quickly said, "You're pretty ballsy there, Quiñonez. What are you doing?"

"Just looking for a hot guy," he responded. I chuckled at his boldness and didn't quite know what to say.

I began to think about how different I had become, more so even in the past year. How these stupid little instances had happened to me in the past and how maybe under different circumstances I would have continued our conversation to see where things would lead. But I had now been given a different perspective on life; a clearer picture in which to frame the situation I was currently in.

I looked into his eyes and told him that I had just ended a relationship with someone who inadvertently and unknowingly changed my life completely. I let him know that I appreciated his attention and told him to be safe, that one day he'll know what I was talking about. He agreed and I turned around to face another hill. I heard him grip his handlebars a few moments after my initial steps in the opposite direction and the "thud, thud" from his tires soon became fainter and fainter.

I couldn't help but think of Judy and our prophetic afternoon teatime conversations. It was so firmly imprinted in my mind, and by now things were coming into fruition in surprising ways. I didn't want to go back to NYC and face another day of waiting for life to begin again. I had been looking for something to point me in the right direction for a long time, but nothing was surfacing that would give me any indication of which next steps to take besides a far-off vision of the life I was supposed to live. I accepted the fact that it was all up to me in the end.

I picked up a dried leaf from the ground and heard another crackle of thunder approaching. The storm was making its way toward the park, so I walked up the last remaining hill to the parking lot, and into the air-conditioned comfort of my car.

I looked in the rear-view mirror and realized that the person I left behind was the man I used to be. I had been so confused; waiting for someone to save me and looking for someone to save. I started her up, turned on the radio, and watched the rain on the windshield drizzle and drip in front of me.

False Advertising

Living with frat boys for a summer was yet another up-close-and-personal view into the frightening lifestyle of the young, straight male; the likes of which I will never forget, no matter how much electroshock therapy I will endure. The countless sleepless nights, the sounds of screaming at 2:30 in the morning, wild party girls slamming their high heel shoes on the hardwood floor like dancing elephants, being woken up by a vomiting stranger in my bathroom. It felt more like a revolving-door frat party than a "Fully Furnished Bedroom with Shared Utilities" as advertised on Craigslist.

One sleepless night, I decided to buy cleaning supplies from the local Wal-Mart. I mopped the floors by five in the morning, disinfected the bathrooms by seven, and called it a day by nine. I got used to living the schedule of a third-shift janitor.

Sandals were a necessity and part of an itemized list I deducted from rent. I guess it didn't matter because anything spotted or splattered with an article of food or bodily fluid tended to blend into the circa '78 wallpaper with speckled fruit and tiny butter-cream flowers. Hardly the type of thing you'd expect to find in a primo bachelor pad, but something I found solace in during my time in Hell. Dancing dolphins on stained-glass windows were contrasted by a broken front door that Travis ripped off its hinges in a fit of alcohol-induced rage, and red leather couches placed around the room to cover up human head-sized holes in the walls.

I worked security at Target and found myself making frequent trips to the health and beauty aisle just so I could get a few free squirts of the new lotion testers. The week before, I waxed everything that an Asian esthetician would legally pull off my body for a hundred and fifty bucks. I felt like a naked cat shivering in my well air-conditioned bedroom, rather than an old sheep dog I had grown accustomed to naturally consider myself. It had been a very long time since I could remember feeling so young. My legs were smoother than my head; one of the few places on my body that didn't grow much hair.

Unbuttoning my uniform to lubricate my freshly plucked chest and making sure not to miss the backs of my knees, I would look from one end of the isle to the other to make sure no one was looking. I'd make my way back to the office in time to buy a box of popcorn and a soda from the food court. My manager played back the security tape of my personal moisturizing session and I barely got off with a warning for indecent exposure.

It was bad enough that no one respected the fact that a guy as non-threatening looking as me was there to enforce the law. The amount of training it took to become a mall cop made it worse--hardly worth nine dollars an hour before taxes. I patrolled the store with my best Clint Eastwood impersonation and spent most of my days looking over surveillance footage of the parking lot and docks. I would call myself on my walkie-talkie, pretending I was chasing after a hardened criminal just so I could look busy and important. I stayed there until I got a yoga teaching scholarship in the mountains that year. I gladly put in my two weeks-notice, and turned in my plastic, silver nametag.

I hardly saw my roommates sober. I don't know how I would have reacted if I had. I cultivated more of a pissed-off sympathy for them than anything, so given that we differed so much in our definitions of what it meant to be human, I decided to skip the "getting to know you" phase of our relationship and to consider the experience: "Straight Camp for the Gay Guy."

Palmetto bugs made their way through the holes in our screens and into my closet that housed the stash of dry goods I had to conceal from the boys since they kept eating all my food. I would wake up to find a box of pasta strewn across the floor and a jar of half-eaten peanut butter artfully hidden in the back of the fridge as if trying to erase any evidence of thievery. I'd leave a cup of freshly prepared lemonade in the fridge and would think twice about retrieving it later after hearing Travis's story about the time he was high and mistook his fridge for a toilet.

I guess my passive aggressive tactics didn't help matters after that. Eating Eric's spicy buffalo wings from Hooters and drinking Travis's three-liter bottle of Diet Sprite was one thing. But taking a heaping spoonful of peanut butter and placing it on top of a pile of Sam's white laundry didn't drive my point home any clearer. You'd think that my leaving post-it notes around the kitchen like "Dan's Food--POISONED--May Cause Anal Leakage" would deter them. Instead, it inspired them to continue conducting acts of burglary while I was hard at work pretending to catch bad guys.

Sleeping on the couch downstairs then became more of a necessity than an option. It meant that the bugs in my closet couldn't find me in bed and that my nightmares would be hushed by popping in a DVD on their enormous, flat-screen television with super surround sound and seat subwoofers. I was hoping it would also stop the boys from having loud, obnoxious parties that would undoubtedly have to be broken up by the Raleigh police department. No such luck. I had to resort to more evolved tactics of aversion.

One night, to keep what little pride I had left, I decided to eat a slew of Chinese food after working out. I thought it would give me the runs after my step-aerobics class at the local YMCA. I proceeded to relieve myself in our communal commode putting caution tape over the closed doorframe for added measure.

I fell asleep around 1:30 in the morning and woke up around noon the same day. When I woke up, no one was at home and I had no idea if my plan had worked or not because I had a splitting headache and couldn't bear to open the blinds that were broken and tacked with blankets to keep out any light. It was the best night's sleep I'd gotten in a while and the boys were totally MIA.

A part of me was paranoid that they realized what a crime scene I had left for them and may have called the National Guard to come in and nuke the place, but I remembered them saying something about going to the mountains for a friend's bachelor party. I checked Eric's Beach Babes calendar in his room and saw that they, in fact, did leave and would be returning after Memorial Day weekend.

I spent the rest of the weekend cleaning up the remnants of my dastardly plan of ultimate revenge and bought them new groceries to boot. When they came home, they were so happy that I took care of everything in their absence that their fist-punch of gratitude was enough to soften the blow. I was the hero of the day, so they decided to lay off the wet willies for the time being. With a mop in one hand and a bright, rubber glove in the other, I proceeded to smile and finish spraying the countertops with Fantastik.

My only worry was that Eric would realize that I smoked all his weed that weekend. I had forged a note from Travis that read, "I owe u, Dude!" I doubted either one of them would remember or care, so I took a breath knowing that no matter what, I had gotten my revenge. In the end I guess I learned that stooping to their level was just more hassle than it was worth.

The Window Washer

It was just another job on a hot summer afternoon. I trudged up the stairs with my big red bucket full of cleaning supplies banging my bare calves with each step--sweat dripping from my pores--and a lowly smile burning in the sun. I kept hold of the idea that making money was a good thing no matter what honest work I had to do. Most people were inside their homes going about their days, reading books, and watching TV, while I was out on a ladder balancing a windowpane with one foot while swatting a mosquito with a towel. I had joined the bandwagon of the misfortunate ones whose preeminent occupation consisted of laborious tasks that no one with enough money would dare do if they could help it.

I painted sheds, cleaned spider webs, swept walkways of debris, and sprayed insecticides and weed killers on grass in dark, scary corners under patios. I washed cars and drove delivery trucks, cleaned windows, vacuumed floors, painted rooms, and made flower arrangements by the thousands. I wrote a few school papers for students who would eventually drop out and transcribed verbatim the mumblings of corporate executives. I was a temp at a big-time modeling agency in New York City, a receptionist extraordinaire who could type a bazillion words a minute on someone else's clock. I mowed lawns, baby-sat, kid-sat, adult-sat, cat-sat, dog-sat, fish-sat, apartment-sat, house-sat, condo-sat…you name it I eventually sat on it.

I painted houses, cleaned windows, moved furniture twice my size, raked leaves, cleaned pools, planted flowers, donated blood, and sang and danced all for money. I waited tables and told a few jokes, never knowing it would come to pass for anything more than passing time and paying the bills.

I even played background piano for a group of people giving a lecture on the health benefits of sex. I had a hard time concentrating on the pedals that night. My foot kept slipping when I'd turn my body around to gawk at their visual aids.

Luckily, I never did anything I really hated for any extended period. That just wasn't in my nature. To not do something I loved to the best of my ability was a travesty. I sold greeting cards door to door as a child, learning how to buy low and sell high. My heart was never fully into serving artery-clogging cheese fries or chili cheese potato skins at Hard Times Café. But I did it anyway, because it was all leading up to something, whether I could see it then or not. Old ladies would leave me a few quarters for my kind words about their blouses and orthopedic shoes. I always knew there was something more that I was supposed to do with my life. So the struggle and search continued.

Then, I met Bob and his wife, Phyllis. They lived in what used to be my old voice teacher's weight room. Now, it had been completely remodeled to a comfortable living environment for two retirees who thankfully loved each other's company. They had been married for almost fifty years. Bob had just come down with cancer of the joints and Phyllis was fighting breast cancer without medical intervention of any kind. She simply didn't believe in that sort of stuff. She was going to fight it herself with the power of her mind, heart, and nature. Her wide-set eyes told a gentle story and her husband's grit sang of military adventures on the high seas.

I was contracted to meet Bob at ten in the morning on a Wednesday. He greeted me at the door in an old workout suit complete with a white headband and socks pulled high over his shins. Phyllis was finishing her croissant and had bits of the bread all over her lips, as she smiled wide and spoke kind words with her mouth full. If these were the people I was going to be working for, I should have cancelled my dates for the entire day because I had a feeling it was going to take a while.

Bob's eagerness to get started on the project was quite adorable. It was almost as if he had been waiting for someone to work with him for some time. He was straightforward in his approach, simple with his words, and gentle in his intention. I could feel a calm hush over me as Phyllis popped open water bottles for both of her afternoon heroes. Bob and I went right to work.

Bob was set on working close with me, so I gave him the inside and I worked willingly in the heat. I didn't know if this was to save money, or to make sure that I was doing the job to his tight specifications. Either way, I didn't mind his company and the fact that I had someone else there to save me from making two trips inside and outside the air-conditioning was a comfort no matter how much longer the job would take.

We worked for hours, each one going by faster than the other. It took thirty minutes to wash one window. Bob needed a lot of breaks, but I didn't mind at all since the air-conditioned basement welcomed me with open arms. We'd sit together on leather patio chairs and clean the larger panes by hand. We hardly spoke except to pass along items and tools to complete the job, but it was remarkable how much I got from him without saying a word.

* * *

Growing up I hardly got to see my father. When I did, the time spent together was never utilized as a positive demonstration of what being a man entailed. All I knew was that a man was supposed to work all the time, marry a woman who demeaned him every chance she got, and make jokes during serious conversations. As a young child there were some gentler times where he would read to us and tickle the piggies on our feet.

When he was around he would lay down in the middle of the floor in our bedroom. Both Erik and my beds were on opposite sides of the room and dad would hold both of our hands until we fell asleep. I never fell asleep though. I didn't trust it. I always had to see him leave and close the door behind him before I allowed myself to drift off. Like most trusting children, Erik was asleep in no time. I found his ability endearing.

Dad told us stories about our uncle, the ninja plumber from Yonkers, that always had us in stitches. I would take over the storytelling after a while and make the bad guy get chased down the street by one of Erik's signature turds. My little brother only ate white bread, Pepsi, and corn, and sometimes would forget to flush the toilet. Surprised at the sight that lay beneath me while peeing, I could have sworn that they were those miniature chocolate eggs you'd get from CVS or Walgreens during their 40% off Easter sales.

Misty, one of our innumerable, domesticated, feral felines, got into the toilet one afternoon and began playing with one of my younger brother's poopsickles on the beige, shag carpet in the hallway that led to the playroom. I couldn't tell what they were at first, so I ran upstairs to analyze them under a microscope with the chemistry set I got for Christmas. I noticed Misty bouncing off the walls, scared by my hyperactive leap to the top of the stairs. I looked at Misty's tracks that were all over the walls and carpet and couldn't understand how she got that close to the ceiling. But then, Misty was always one of those special cats that emulated the phrase "Bless her heart," and would wail in heat at 3 in the morning even though she was properly spayed. It was an anomaly that we just learned to throw pillows at and accept.

I walked slowly to the bathroom dividing my attention between the crime scene in the hallway and the toilet bowl lid. The smell of undigested corn and yeast caught me off guard, so I focused my energy on devising a creative solution to explain what had just transpired. It was the only way a creative kid like me could tolerate being alone for so long.

I didn't have a lot of guidance at home. Although, our dynamic lacked structure, there was always the television to instill the kinds of valuable life lessons learned from normal, conscientious parenting. Most of my values derived from watching programs like *Reading Rainbow* and *The Facts of Life*. I longed to be a Huxstable on *The Cosby Show* and to jump rope with the pastor from *Amen,* discussing life lessons such as when to say no to drugs and how to ruefully avoid parking tickets. As I got older, I looked for those opportunities in other places and I found them in a lot of other men and women like teachers and wise, random strangers.

* * *

Phyllis called Bob from downstairs and he jumped like something had bit him on the behind. Even though I could hear him very well through the windows, he insisted on using hand gestures to indicate when it was time for lunch or time for a break. From what I gathered of his talking hands and chomping jaws, lunch was ready, and we were probably going to be talking with our mouths full. I was starving and couldn't wait to take a break. The heat was intense, but the mosquitoes were even worse.

Phyllis made sandwiches, chips and dip, and opened up cans of diet coke. I was in Heaven! We chatted about life, politics, and boats. The latter I knew nothing about, so I nodded my head pretending I knew what "starboard" and "tiller" meant.

I asked them questions like, "What can I do to prevent osteoporosis?" and "What would you do differently if you weren't going to die tomorrow?" All questions that stumped them on the first try. But they both took turns speaking and listening just like all the good parenting books tell you to do when communicating with loved ones. They spoke about old memories and things you only see on Hallmark commercials.

I came back to finish the upstairs four days later and thirty minutes late. I had stayed out until three-thirty in the morning after a concert and was a little hung over. I arrived at the door and they greeted me again with open arms. I felt totally guilty. Bob had been ready to work, so I couldn't dilly-dally any longer. We got our materials ready and headed outside. I approached the stairs with my big red bucket and saw that these windows were even larger and more numerous than the other ones. It didn't matter, because I wanted to spend time with Bob and eat more of Phyllis's food. That was incentive enough to keep my mouth shut and finish the job.

We started in the back this time and worked our way toward the front. Bob showed me a few tricks he had learned from his years of home repairs, like how to apply grout with chopsticks and how to clean the bathroom with just orange peels and a lemon. There were moments when I didn't think we'd ever finish, but I just looked at the old man with that white headband and high-ribbed socks and just smiled with sincere appreciation.

When I had to use the ladder and he would tell me through the glass to be careful and to keep my weight close to the house, not to shift my weight too far away or to stand on the top rung. I was standing directly above giant shrubs the size of mid-size SUVs and would invariably be pierced through the heart by a branch if I had fallen. He saw that I began to understand what I was doing, but nevertheless it made him feel better reminding me as much as possible. I appreciated that because he knew I could do the task but was still looking out for me. Hardly the kind of positive reinforcement I was used to.

Phyllis prepared sandwiches again, cheese and crackers and homemade oatmeal-raisin cookies. Again, I was in Heaven! We spoke about many things like where they'd traveled together, what I'd been up to in New York, and why I was washing windows. Of course, our conversations would never be complete without a shocker or two.

Phyllis mentioned to me that after a few glasses of wine she can read palms and "see things." I mentioned that after a few hits of marijuana I also had spiritually enlightening experiences. Just when I thought I'd get an, "Okay, it's time for you to go!" they were pleasantly intrigued and asked me a few questions about the subject. There was a little silence and then Phyllis openly told me about the one time she smoked "that stuff."

Back in the Sixties, she was over at a girlfriend's house and her friend "...pulled out a pipe that you put liquid in and smoke it." I attested that the item she was describing was a bong and she replied, "Oh, yes...a bong...that's right" and continued with her story:

"...en sow ay took this pieep, this bahng, and smoked et en ay cood a danced al nieet! Oh, gosh. Ay was al over tha plaeec. I saw things. Ya know?"

"Yes, I know. What did you see?"

"I sa Gad. He sed ta me, 'What the hell are ya doin thar, Phyllis, tek yar damn hands af that thing and get gooin! An so I did."

"...and so, you did?"

"It was todaly ahsum!"

Bob covered his head as I smiled into the squeaky-clean windows above us.

A Southern, Yankee Boy in Shantytown

Living in Jamaica was a gift from God. I had gotten the opportunity to work with a company that sent fitness experts overseas to teach classes at upscale resorts. My contract was at the Ritz Carlton Resort and Spa in Montego Bay and was only supposed to last for a week. Nothing I'd experienced prior could have prepared me for how transformative living abroad would be. It was something I never thought I'd witness, and something I was determined not to take for granted.

Life had become somewhat normal for me living at one of the finest hotel chains in the world. I woke up early each morning to teach a power-walk class, then I'd shower and slathered suntan lotion on my body before lounging about the pool area for an hour or two. For lunch, I ate freshly caught salmon, aromatic jasmine rice, steamed vegetables, and a delicate slice of carrot cake for dessert topped with pineapple sorbet and a condensed milk, mango drizzle. The sun was beating down on me like an Alabama homophobe as I proceeded to hike up my swimming trunks to work hard on my tan line.

I came back to my hotel room and noticed that Dandelion had turned down my bed and left the flat screen on to my favorite channel, the one with crashing ocean waves and squawking seagulls. I prepared to teach a late afternoon yoga class to dolled-up housewives and a few eager executives escaping a midlife crisis for a little island R&R. That night there was going to be a Jamaican Independence Day festival, and I was to have an up close and personal view of the fireworks by the sea.

As the Caribbean sun plunged into the horizon, there was a reggae band playing by the jerk shack and loads of guests drinking, eating, and smoking God knows what. I sat off to the side from view at a vacant picnic table, watching everyone as if it was the first time I'd been outdoors. I was just mesmerized by the colors, the smells, and the breeze. My senses still couldn't get used to the fact that I was living on my own version of an island paradise.

To my left was a couple smooching, then a family of three seated directly in front of them grooving to the music wearing matching tie-dye Bob Marley shirts and a wig of dreadlocks. The band slowly jammed as the effects of ganja started to kick in like a mellow haze all around me.

Suddenly, the singer asked if anyone wanted to come up and sing a song. I buried my head in my neck since I was never good at performing songs that did not required a month's notice and weeks of rehearsal time. I could stand up in front of millions of people I didn't know and perform something I'd thoroughly rehearsed, but if it wasn't showtunes or a choral piece I was pretty much screwed.

A drunk, British guy got up on the stage. He was a crew member with a bunch of flight attendants who were in port for the weekend. Without warning he walked on stage and began to rock out to "Sittin' on the Dock of the Bay." I slowly eased my way onto the dance floor, transfixed by the mirage of beauty that stood four feet above me. His colleagues, still in their airline uniforms, were the liveliest group I'd seen on the island in a month.

What really shocked me was that I was witnessing my first openly gay man in Jamaica fling his arms up and recite the words in full force, "Sittin' on Your Cock Everyday..." I was never so happy to hear such profanity in all my life. "They do exist!"

After I listened to the man sing, I wondered how long he was in town. I began to contemplate buying a one-way ticket to England, just to see if he could help adjust my tray table. I went back to my room to change into something more appropriate. A full-fledged evening gown, and a pink hibiscus flower positioned between my ear and temple would have been a bit too much, even though I had already bought the matching pumps.

I didn't want one of my people seeing me in running shorts and a tank top at a an Independence Day Reggae dance party. I had to look beach bum cool, like I was an expat who had been living on the island for years. Kinda like I had a social life but was way too cool to wear anything constricting like shoes.

I looked through my barren closet and chose a pair of long, khaki shorts with lots of pockets and zippers at the seams, a cap with the logo "Red-Stripe" on the front and my lucky black tank top to accentuate my rippling tanned physique. That was my signature island outfit and some of the very few items of clothing I owned.

Before I left for Jamaica, my aunt gave me a bag full of my cousin's used athletic attire. She told me that if I was going to be living on an island where homosexuality was practically punishable by death, I'd better buy some straight guy clothes or kiss the rest of my crazy life goodbye. So, I forwent the tight, fitted jeans for baggy basketball shorts that almost went down to my ankles.

When I got back to the shack, I felt the cool, crunchy sand beneath my bare toes. I watched two little girls run around the dance floor like pretty, little lunatics. Just then the singers beckoned everyone back on the dance floor by playing a great, upbeat number. I gracefully scooted my way onto the dance floor like a smooth operator. After working up a little sweat, we all made our way to the lounge chairs by the shore to watch the fireworks display.

Now as a kid I hated the loud booms, the gut-wrenching anticipation as each crackle echoed in my tiny eardrums, and the fact that no matter how far away I was, I thought I was going to be singled out by that one stray ember and be burned alive. But that night, with the sounds of the Caribbean Sea to my right, all that fear left me, and I sat back on the lounge chair to enjoy the evening's festivities with a smile on my face and a twinkle in my eyes.

The fireworks started and caught everyone by surprise. There were screaming ones, some with short bursts, long bursts--every different color burst--and tons of glittery specks flying every which way in the night air. There were wavy ones and spirally ones and ones that spewed out like lava from a volcano. In childlike amazement, I sat back and watched as each pyrotechnic crackle sprayed its magic over my head in the sky.

When it was all finished, we clapped, and I let the smoke clear before dipping my feet into the lukewarm saltwater. I could see a storm brewing beyond the horizon as the lightning silently zapped the waves in the distance. I turned back to see where my future British husband was, but he was already long gone. Maybe he was on the Hip Strip, sloshed, looking for trouble. Perhaps he was asleep like the rest of his crew, preparing for an early flight the next morning.

Two months had gone by and I was contracted to spend a week at a resort in Negril. I was told to pack light and to make sure I brought a lot of sunscreen. There was this overwhelming feeling that I had no idea what I was getting myself into. Each time I told people where I was going to be spending my week away from the Ritz, their eyebrows rose, and their mouths formed silent "Os."

On the ride over I noticed three things: for every bar there was a church built right next to it; for every stray goat there were three children knocking on cars and begging for money from unsuspecting, White tourists; and air-conditioning was a sincerely under-appreciated luxury. It wasn't uncommon to see people bathing in the beautiful waves that crashed upon the sand. Tall grasses provided shade for those seeking refuge from the sun, as they sat on their rickety porches talking with friends and fanning each other while braiding their children's hair. Stray dogs with their rib cages protruding from empty bellies searched for scraps of food, while feral cats hid cautiously under the cracked foundations of crumbling shacks.

We arrived at Hedo II and were met by a few men with giant smiles on their faces and bulging bellies. They were happy to hand deliver our bags directly to our front doors. If I was with a woman I would have had room service, but since it was clear that I wasn't going to provide any eye candy that week for the men in charge, my bags were dropped onto the driveway by my room, to be picked up later by my next-door neighbors.

Their names were Andy and Kim. They were the brownest-looking White people I'd ever met. They watched porn at full volume, twenty-four hours a day, leaving their doors wide open while they were having wild sex. They knocked on my door, and I answered it with caution, leaving it a crack open with the chain locked in its "I'm here, but I don't want to sleep with you" position. When I finally opened the door, I found them both in their robes looking to enter my room. I thanked them and said that I was having my room inspected for pubic lice.

That evening, I went to the dining room for a hearty meal of stewed oxtail and bammy, while I waited patiently for the evening's festivities to begin. Blaring from the microphone was a group of young natives who began to shimmy and shake their bodies to the beat of their island favorites. Clapping their hands, they had the crowd up and dancing on the floor in no time. I realized I was going to have to wait this one out to get a better perspective of the people I was going to be spending the next six nights with.

I made my way over to the lounge pool for a frozen strawberry margarita and started to strike up a conversation with a group of Americans. Danielle and Raquel were sisters. They both were tall, Black women who reminded me of young Diana Ross. Their friend, China, was a voluptuous, light-skinned Black woman who had the kind of soft, feminine sensuality that made her bedroom eyes impossible to look away from. Their friend and fellow homo was named James. He was a quiet hairdresser who prided himself on his well-maintained braids and the pursed lip look to the side that was made popular by self-photographed female celebrities. These new friends gave me the means to remain as virginal as possible when confronted by the other nudists that week.

That night I went to sleep with earplugs firmly stuffed into my ear canals as Andy and Kim pounded the walls in bliss. Being a New Yorker, I pretended there was an underground subway station just behind my headboard and that Kim's screams were the sirens of an ambulances racing through the streets in order to save a child's life. It left me with the pleasant images I needed for an undisturbed, restful night's sleep.

The next morning, I was scheduled to teach an early afternoon water-aerobics class at the nude beach. I had breakfast in the dining room and met my group of friends from the night before. I told them about Andy and Kim, and they told me, "Just wait. You ain't seen nothin' yet!" This fortuitous message left me something to think about as I pushed sausages around my plate of runny scrambled eggs.

I prepared to teach the aerobics class as I had done for months at the Ritz. This time, however, I would have to be unclothed and even more motivated than before in order to inspire nudists with hangovers to get healthy.

I picked up a rented boom box and my trusty bath towel and made my way over to the nude beach to get a quick tan. It was the first time I'd ever been naked in the daytime in public. Although I looked the fiercest I was ever going to look in my life, I still had reservations about the whole thing. I undressed in the barren part of the beach and began to apply sunscreen to parts of my body that had been fully clothed since before I was in diapers. I jumped onto my raised lounge chair and peered through the white, plastic slats to see who was going to make the first move.

Couples started to trickle in and remove their towels as if they hadn't a care in the world, exposing every part of themselves without hesitation. Once the towels were discarded onto the sand, they reached their arms up into the air to feel the breeze on their nipples and armpits. I curled into a ball and looked up into the sky and prayed for rain.

I took a few deep breaths and stepped onto the beach fully and completely naked. I posed like Michelangelo's "David" and noticed someone glance over my way. I quickly jumped into the water to hide my naughty bits and ended up stepping on something that I later found out was a sea urchin. I had to cancel class that afternoon to visit the nurse.

She took one look at me and said, "Don be a behbeh now, dis ting es jusa splin now. Herr, all bettah now."

With that she had cut into my foot to pull out two little black splinters, and the pain was all over in a matter of seconds. "Don lemme catcha ya gettin dees tings en er ass na, oh-k?" I hung my head, knowing full well she had my room number, and nodded in polite agreement.

For lunch, I headed back to the dining room limping like a maimed duck. I met my friends and who wanted to know how class went. I told them I had to cancel because I got stung by a sea urchin. James asked with a side smile, "Did he get chu in the ass?" Riotous laughter ensued. After things died down, I asked "No, and why the hell is everyone around here so concerned with my ass?" China joined the revelry and poked me in the side a few times before changing subjects.

After our lasagna and vegetable soup, and an intelligible game of Jamaican trivia, I went over to the gym to teach a yoga class. No one showed up and I felt completely useless. I didn't know what my purpose was if no one was going to show up for class. I talked with a guy on one of those workout balls and he said, between sit-ups, "Why donna yuh jus enjar yarself, noh?" Watching the beads of sweat caress his chocolate, rippling abs, I agreed. I smiled and left him losing count and having to regrettably start his ab workout all over again.

I skipped dinner that evening and went back to my bedroom. I unpacked and took my fifth shower in two days. I guess I wanted to make sure I was getting as much off my skin as I could that week. I laid in bed as the day turned into night, then I heard music coming from the dining area, so I put my dress clothes on and went to see what all the fuss was about.

As I was cresting up a hill, I listened to the bugs chirp around me while watching the night sky glisten like one of those planetarium exhibitions on the wonders of the galaxy. The asphalt led to sand and a wooden staircase past the gym on my left. The music was getting louder, and I saw a lot of people dancing and having a good time under the moonlight. They were all dolled up, and I noticed there were themes each night that everyone was privy to, but I wasn't aware of. If I was going to really enjoy myself that weekend, I had better get the low down and fast.

On the dance floor, I met a handful of my friends. After getting exhausted from dancing, we went to the waterslide and noticed a couple of people screaming as they made their way down the long, curving tubes. I told James to check out what I was going to do and he buried his head in his hands.

"Honey, don't chu know what that is? That's a damn, naked-ass water slide. You won't catch me dead goin' down that thang!"

Just then I had a thought. I disrobed slowly as the ladies cheered me on. It was my first impromptu strip tease to inaudible music. Folding my dress shirt and slacks on the patio chair, I tucked my dress shoes and black socks under the seat and chasséd my way up the stairs that lead to the top of the waterslide. I screamed down the tunnel and watched as the colors of light turned from dark red to bright orange and aqua blue as I skimmed the water's surface with my bare ass plunging feet first into the cool, chlorinated water.

I shook myself off and noticed I was completely high off endorphins. I made my way up the stairs again and called out to my friends to come with me. Danielle and Raquel were already taking off their clothes as China and James stayed below smoking marijuana-laced cigarettes. We cheered each other on and had a total blast! When finished, James looked at me--high as a kite--as China sipped a sloshy martini with her pinky high in the air. I dried myself off and we all went back to our respective rooms for the evening.

The next morning I was readier than ever to teach. I had the courage and the mindset to really enjoy myself that week, so I got my little boom box ready and placed my clean, white towel on the floor for traction. I called everyone in the pool to get their friends over to take class. I stood, stark naked in front of about twenty nudists with my hands on my hips like Peter Pan grooving to a make-shift CD of '90s club hits. The music was certainly outdated, but since the average age around the place was above 40, I thought it would get people thinking of their more active, younger years.

Jumping up and down, with my penis flopping to and fro, I punched out jabs and uppercuts like I was Taebo's Billy Blanks at a P-90 Bootcamp class. I started overworking the aged crowd and decided to chill with a relaxing cool-down. After class, I got another frozen strawberry margarita and sat by the water to watch the waves. The sun was beating down on my forehead and I breathed long and hard, loving my newfound freedom.

That night was "fetish night" and I had no idea what the hell I was going to wear. I had no fetishes--at least none that I would outright admit to myself--so, I had to ask my friends what they thought I should do. I stopped in the doorway of their room.

James had on a skimpy leather outfit, while Raquel had only a whip in her hand. Danielle had a baby doll costume on, and China looked like a giant, sexy cat. I had my trusty black tank top on and my tried-and-true basketball shorts that were ripped and shredded where it counted. I was pulled into the room as the redneck White boy in desperate need of a makeover.

They proceeded to dress me up and I ended up wearing thick black, platform heels, laced all the way up my waxed calves with black satin ribbons, tiny bikini briefs held together by two small bits of black elastic, and two of James's hair bands that fit tightly around my stomach and chest. China had an extra naughty kitten eye mask that I tied around my ears to hide my anxiety. I looked fierce, but the green apple blowpop didn't stay tucked between the thin elastic bands for very long.

After taking first prize in both the costume competition and the dance competition, I went to the beach with my friends to watch the stars and talk about life. James pulled out a joint and started passing it around. Knowing I was in good company and not wanting to go back to the States without partaking in a communal smoke session in the marijuana capital of the world, I took a deep, long puff and sat back on the lounge chair next to James and China. We told stories of our lives and our most hilarious mistakes and personal triumphs. After noticing the sun coming up in the distance, we dizzily made our way back to our rooms to purge ourselves of our sins under running tap water.

After teaching another water aerobics class, I tanned for a bit and decided to move the yoga class to a rock by the water. I advertised that a naked yoga class was going to be taking place at 4 p.m. that day and would last for approximately an hour and a half. I doubted anyone would show up, but I was going to try it anyway. Four p.m. rolled by and no one came to class. Perhaps I was too ambitious with my lengthy workout request. With the Caribbean sun behind me, I began to salute the Universe with my naked dedication to the mind, body, and spirit connection. The entire experience was breathtaking!

The day we all had to leave, everyone at the resort was both hung-over and very sad to be leaving a place that was so freeing and accepting of everyone's differences. Granted there were only three gay people there, I was the only one who could admit it in public, but I'm sure there was no other place in Jamaica that I could even have dreamed of being that open with people. My friends and I sat at the big, round table, and exchanged information to hopefully keep in touch. They told me that if I was going to write about them that I'd better make them all "bold, Black, and beautiful." I promised that I'd do my best and thanked them.

There was a tradition that those who were staying at the resort had to moon their friends who were leaving for the airport. I was headed to the Ritz but had to catch a connecting bus back to the hotel. When our bus started rolling away from the parking lot, I glanced over and saw about ten faces peeking back at me preparing to duck under the bushes for my farewell moon. Ten butts, all in a row, shined their derrières in my general direction shaking their cheeks from side to side like bobble-heads.

I touched the window and watched each of them for as long as I could. I had just experienced the best week of my life, and now it was back to work. I turned my head and looked forward to the road that would take most of us home. I clutched my yoga mat and closed my eyes, silently laughing at myself for already missing those crazy folks.

Back to Life

I used to write with such ease at grandma's house. There was so much inspiration for a budding, cynical wordsmith. Much like lovers excited by the prospect of getting caught, I expected grandma to find me masturbating words of hope onto a computer screen in the darkened abyss that was my Puerto Rican aunt's childhood bedroom. After arriving back to the States, I was quickly settling back into the swing of reality in the Bronx with my beloved dog, Charlie.

Aida hadn't been home for many months and I'd taken the liberty of keeping her house warm during the long, grueling winter. After spending three hours cleaning the gelatinous muck out of her stale refrigerator and throwing roach motels down into the basement like grenades, I backed off my domestic duties for a while to play with Charlie. I wanted to make sure he wasn't going to be scarred for life while he was living there, so I sprayed everything down that had a surface, wiping off years of sediment and grime. Charlie thought nothing of his new environment and began sniffing around for buried treasure. He stood ready to play; his tongue hanging off to the sides of his jowls in anticipation of roughhousing.

Before leaving for Jamaica, he was still a pup and even though his godmother (Cindy) in Raleigh sent me pictures of him resting regally on a pink, embroidered settee, I still had to see the changes with my own eyes to appreciate how much he had grown in the past four months. Cindy was the most amazing godmother for Charlie, and if it wasn't for her and her husband, Carl, I don't know what we would have done. A gigantic Labrador with the energy of a puppy made rounding tight corners something to reconsider during the training process. Still, I loved every inch of him with all my heart.

When his tail would wag so would his rear-end. Both would go in opposite directions, and the sight reminded me of when water balloons are dropped on the floor from a slippery grip. The occasional passing of gas was abhorrently uncomfortable for my guests, but his eager mug and floppy ears made my heart sing. I was happy to be his daddy again, even though we both were much different than before.

After spending four months in Jamaica, I learned a few valuable lessons: never commit a crime on the island or no one you love would hear from you again, make sure that you stocked up on digestive enzymes before entering the curried, coconut world that is Jamaican cuisine, and when in Jamaica make sure you learn how to wait or else you are doomed in a country that has no concept of time.

Life in Jamaica was slow, even when it was fast. There was a sense that time ultimately stood still and the more one challenged that system the more troublesome life had the potential of becoming. It was an island full of religion, exotic beauty, and an inclination that everything was going to be just fine no matter what the circumstances. It was the land of Bob Marley and vigilante justice.

Upon my return to the States, I was thrilled to go back to my regular diet of hearty, fibrous wheat toast and grilled chicken salads. However, I realized I had developed a peculiar allergy to wheat and tomatoes while away. It seemed that my body was revolting against leaving a natural paradise for the gloomy "island" of taxis and hotdog stands.

Without complaint, I realized rather quickly that luxury was just that. I was going to relish the memories of meals delivered to me via room service at the Ritz, prepared with a friendly smile by native islanders with nametags reading "Thadison" or "Penelope." Under their care and supervision, my bubble baths and full body waxes came a distant second to our one-on-one chats about Jamaican island culture on the veranda.

With the sun reflecting off tiny, neon-yellow tennis balls being bounced from one leisurely tennis player to another, Thadison and I would sit listening to the sounds of crashing waves feet from my hotel room. The smell of salt water and lavender wafted by as groundskeepers trimmed hibiscus flowers off the bushes for use in teas and in foyer decorations. Some would happily pluck coconuts off the trees for thirsty guests, pulling out their machetes for a crowd full of gasping spectators and popping off the tops with one, clean chop.

Yes, I knowingly agreed to relinquish my throne and to put two feet firmly upon the ground to breathe the toxic fumes of the big, bad city once more. I found myself sitting in grandma's old chair. Her comfortable, form fitted, beige lazy-boy and the small, quilted pillow, now weathered from age and overuse.

My laptop sat warming my thighs and Charlie laid sleeping soundly beneath my feet. I had bags and boxes all around me, and the lights were lit enough for me to see a few words scroll across the computer screen. I peered out the small, dark windows as car lights flashed by, streaming along the barren walls of grandma's living room like searchlights in the star-spangled sky.

There were pictures of my extended family and myself as a confused, pre-teen boy in small, shiny frames on the cold, stone coffee table. Everything had dust caked on it. Even the dust was dusty.

Tucked in a corner behind a stack of crinkled, outdated TV Guides was an old-fashioned accordion-like piano that blew sound when certain buttons were pressed. I remembered placing my delicate fingers across the keyboard when I was very young. Now it was forced to stand upright resting against the wall for all of eternity.

I noticed the wooden floors I used to tip toe across as a child, scared of my grandmother's wrath. I remembered the smell of pizza boxes being brought in from the cold night air by my father, and the most delicious Chinese food sailing into the hallway in white plastic bags with smiley faces on them. The smell of rice and beans, vinegar and oils, and the Adobo seasoning glazed on my grandfather's chicken were still ever-present in my memory. Not to mention the plastic couches we would eventually stick to after passing out from regrettable gluttony.

I sat and noticed how empty the house felt. How the only life I knew now was Charlie, me, and the vermin who called this place home. I leaned a little farther back in grandma's comfy chair and began to let my thoughts drift. With so much already lived through, there was still so much more I'd yet to even consider knowing fully. Charlie scratched his ears and shook more fur onto the dirty, soot-ridden rug. Staring back at me, he wondered when I was going to get the hint that he wanted to play. A few seconds later, he curled into a tight ball, nestling his cold, wet nose into his tail, and quickly drifted off to sleep.

Poked in the Eye by Lust

I honestly never thought adulthood was going to be such a shitty, responsible mess. I thought life was supposed to be like an '80s movie, where I'd be met at the senior prom by a smitten Andrew McCarthy and be whisked off my feet with a misty, nighttime kiss. Then, I'd mistakenly wish my baby brother away, and--in a puff of glitter, smoke, and spandex--David Bowie would appear to invite us on a magical journey toward the center of the Labyrinth. Later, my friends and I would discover the body of Chester Copperpot before narrowly escaping the Fratellis in the caverns of a surprisingly adventurous sewer system in Oregon. Sadly, Mr. McCarthy never returned my phone calls, so I decided to set my sights on the dashing Cary Elwes.

Back then, I prided myself on steadfast convictions when it came to the more creative aspects of life. An unwavering ability to hold on to an innocent, childlike view of reality had gotten me through some sticky situations. I had little care for most matters of popular concern, which is how I trudged through the mud without a clump of clay on my Kenneth Cole shoes. I liked to call this uncanny knack: "resiliency in the face of adversity." At least that's what I'd like to see written on my tombstone after I die. Instead, it will probably read something like: "The only man who's never been shitted on by a pigeon in front of anyone important."

Yet I must say that at that point in my life I was--for lack of a better cliché--at wits end. I had never felt so stressed out in all my life. I had no idea how to get out from underneath the burdensome, sequined veil I donned to hide my glistening eyes. It was as if the whole world was closing in on me and no repetitive daily affirmation or ass-crack-of-dawn, Ashtanga yoga class seems to be helping. "No, in fact I'm not at peace, I don't feel like a beacon of light or prosperity and I'm not sure, but I think I may have pulled a very important muscle in my groin!"

Still, there was always a glimmer of hope at the end of the rainbow and no hardship ever endures forever. That's what the Do-It-Yourself-Help books say anyway. There were moments when the sun shined through a crack in the clouds. I would catch a ray of light and hold on to it for as long as I was able. However, the weather in my life was usually overcast skies with a high probability of acid rain, and I seemed to find myself stuck behind some asshole swerving uncontrollably into oncoming traffic.

So I kissed the crucifix that hung from my rear-view mirror, like a good recovering Catholic, and tapped the dashboard three times saying, "There's no mace at home, there's no place like Rome, there's no…what?" And in a flash, it was gone. You didn't know if you were dead or alive, but your penis was slowly becoming erect, and you felt a warm, throbbing sensation throughout your lower appendages. Someone you didn't know--but were starting to like--was massaging your prostate whispering in your ear, "Everything's going to be just fine."

Then, I woke up, only to realize I was the only one in control of whether I was going to make it out of this thing alive. Somewhere back in the early '90s I knew that "…the hardest thing to learn was the least complicated." I felt like Nancy Kerrigan and some bitch had just blown apart my kneecap, destroying my entire ice-skating career, and I was left on the ice bawling, "Why? Why? Oh, Why?"

I guess the obvious answer would be to do a Campbell's soup commercial and awkwardly guest-star a few times on *Saturday Night Live*. But what did the not-so-famous person do when they had a fall from grace? Set up residency on their best acquaintance's foldout couch, watching re-runs of *Grey's Anatomy* and eating tubs of Breyer's Mint Chocolate Chip ice cream. No, that would be admitting defeat and I just couldn't let myself do that no matter how much I preferred McDreamy over McSteamy.

Speaking of lust, have you ever been so infatuated with someone that you automatically turn into another person altogether in their presence? Some blabbering idiot who can't even formulate a cohesive sentence? Perhaps you fake a neck spasm to look away from their soul-penetrating gaze? There was one such person in my life that irrevocably had me at "...Cocktail?"

Like Rudolph Valentino, he possessed this alluring way of slicing straight through you with a single movement of his eyes. His name was Michael. He was a tall, dark, and handsome man who poured organic wine at a vegan restaurant at night to pay his way through law school. Yeah...I know.

I wrote a letter one night after obsessing over him for a couple of months and put it in an envelope, sealing it with far too much saliva. With spit dripping down my arm, I made my way into the restaurant with a book and my envelope in hand. The book was my only defense against him; the man which no one could resist.

I took a deep breath before walking past the window of the established Upper East Side hot spot. Pretending like I had just come out of the curtain onto a fabulously lit stage, I steadied myself to perform my most important scene yet: the one of a dim-witted fool poked in the eye by lust.

"Table for one?" a middle-aged woman promptly asked, who reminded me much of Meryl Streep.

"Yes, Darling. A seat at the bar would be divine," I exclaimed in my best frou-frou accent.

She smiled as if humoring a paraplegic at a piano recital and escorted me to my seat. Michael was busy squeezing lychee into a gleaming metal shaker. I took out my book and set aside the envelope that by this time had soaked through the paper due to my overacting salivation glands and sweaty palms.

A young server who was walking past me at the time noticed my envelope and exclaimed, "Oh, Sir, excuse me. I do believe that there was some moisture on the bar and it may have dampened your work. Would you like me to get you another envelope from our office?"

I stared at him with a sideways scoop, as if immediately shocked by jolting electricity. With wide, terrified eyes and a sickly smile, I cleared my throat and tried not to crack my voice, which by this time was slowly transgressing into adolescence from utter embarrassment.

"I'm fine," I eventually squeaked out in a tight, painful whisper.

The server turned around and ran back to the kitchen, visibly shaken, as if fleeing some fatal car crash. Meryl quickly walked past him and mumbled something in vegan; I couldn't quite make it out no matter how much I was leaning in to hear their conversation.

"Can I get you anything, Sir? A glass of wine…cocktail?"

I started to speak, then turned my head to face the bar, "No, I'm waiting for sssssuuuu…" I was speechless. No, I was dumbfounded. I had almost climaxed in my tighty-whities. Not only had he completely undressed me with one look, but he appeared to be aware of my compromising position: the guilty eavesdropper, Meryl the hostess and a young Boy George.

"I think she looks like Meryl Streep…What do you think?"

I did everything in my power not to leap over the bar and attack him from head to toe with my tongue like some ravaging beast, tracing every inch of his body with my lips like uncharted territory.

“I suppose,” I peeped and coughed. Then, I excused myself to the bathroom to splash cold water on my face. Looking into the mirror for a pep talk, I wiped the water from my eyes and fixed what was left of my hair, making sure that my zipper was securely zipped, and my bulge was well apparent. Walking out, I looked past the bar and noticed that my envelope was missing.

I stopped dead in my tracks on the non-slip mat by the doorway into the kitchen causing a three-waiter head-on collision. A hefty sum of glassware and already prepared entrees went showering to the floor. Luckily no one was injured except my pride. The fiasco left Meryl in a tizzy, but thankfully no food had gotten on my one and only good blazer I had saved for special occasions like that night.

I had worn it to two weddings, a funeral, and most recently a divorce party on Fire Island. It still smelled like saltwater and sweat. I felt awful, but luckily Michael was too busy to notice the catastrophe. I escaped with minimal attention when it counted most.

I made my way over to the bar, brushing off bits of glass and tofu noticing Michael keying in a payment at the cash register. “Thank God,” I whispered under my breath. Now I’d have time to get back to my seat, bury my head in the book, order a glass of wine, “accidentally” leave my envelope calligraphically addressed to one *Michael* and get the hell out of there as quickly as possible.

He finished up and was closing the check cover when I reached down to retrieve my envelope, as I had planned it in my mind a thousand times before. I noticed it was gone. I had gotten so frazzled by the previous snafu that I had totally forgot it wasn’t there when I last looked. I had no idea what to do and once again looked like a chicken with my head cut off.

I kept thinking of the lines I had written the night before. The one about, "How I long to feel your warmth on my bare skin, your hands gliding up and down every curve and contour of my landscape; to watch you as your eyes gently close, your body trembles and your lips press ever so slightly upward into a satisfied smile." What if someone found it and was reading it right now in the coat check room, laughing and showing it to all the other servers in the restaurant?

"Oh, my God. My cover is blown. I'm doomed!"

"Excuse me, Sir? You dropped this." The young waiter from before handed me the letter like a child handing his father a report card, with trepidation and dutiful cower. Before thinking, I snatched it out of his hands and put it in between the open pages of Christopher Isherwood's *The Berlin Stories*. I slammed the book shut and ran out of the restaurant as fast as I could.

As I feverishly made my way down 3rd Avenue, I slowly realized how stupidly I had just acted. I was a grown man who was obviously fixated on someone who didn't even know I existed. Plus, I had just terrorized Boy George, pissed off Meryl Streep, and ruined three waiters' otherwise flawlessly served night.

I stopped around 2nd Avenue and looked up at the moon. It was bright and somewhat shady in spots, almost like translucent, smoky clouds were covering a perfect circle of light. I put my hands to my knees and took a breath, looking hard at the gum-spackled pavement.

Walking back to Lexington like a pouting child, I stopped just before the doorway that led into the restaurant. With my back against the wall, I opened the letter and read it to myself.

Yet I sit. I drink my wine and read my book, inconspicuously peering over the pages like a tiger stalking his prey, watching your every movement as if you were the only one in the room; and still between curious gestures of flirtation and coquettishly meeting eyes, there is never an exchange of outright intentions...

I skipped to the bottom and read out loud: "Weren't you the least bit curious as to what I would do to you if given the opportunity?"

I closed my eyes, looked up at the moon and laughed at myself with a wide grin of painful amazement. Oh, my God! How stupid was I? My every perfected word had somehow turned out to be complete and utter horseshit. I didn't even know this guy and I was completely, head-over-heels in love with him. I had built him up in my mind to be this superhero, when he was just some guy trying to make an honest buck.

I looked up at the moon and this time the gray clouds had passed from sight. The clear, shiny circle of light was the only thing visible in the dark sky.

Fireworks

Our life had become fashionably consistent over the many months. However, Anthony's landlord wanted his liver on a plate, and I had just been kicked out of a graduate program for failure to comply. I decided to see a psychiatrist named Serge who would hopefully help me curtail my ineptitude at normalcy, making me more considerate of people I felt were egregiously delusional and less gung-ho about saving the world from imminent disaster. But my personal situation at the time would prove otherwise. What took me a while to accept was that I was the one that was going to be taking a pill every day, not them.

Anthony's apartment was approximately 285 square feet. Subtract from that a handful of headless mannequins, a large drafting table, four injurious stools, an expensive foldout couch he called "The Cappalini," and a full-sized bed he made from plywood and metal. Without a working stove, I would cook three square meals a day in the microwave and cut vegetables with a butter knife on the kitchen hand towel. Somehow, we managed.

Charlie usually nestled next to the radiator on a bed we made for him out of a menagerie of fabrics Anthony had collected from his many years in the fashion industry. Each night we would pull his nest out from underneath The Capalini revealing a furball of organza and chiffon. Only the best for a dog with two dads.

We would wake up each morning around 7:30 a.m. I'd take a shower, walk Charlie by 8am, and make us breakfast by 9. Anthony would sweep the floors and make the bed, while I cleaned Charlie's paws and pretended like I was happy about all of it. Somehow, we would meet for fifteen minutes to watch the morning news before his assistant came to work around 9:30 a.m. Our lives ran like a well-oiled machine. Each night we fell asleep in each other's arms while recounting the day's events.

It was all business as usual until Charlie decided to pee on the floor or eat one of Anthony's pattern pieces. Anthony, seven years my senior, would often find himself in strange predicaments. He'd jam his finger in the old-fashioned bedroom window or swallow an apple peel down the wrong pipe and look at me like a five-year-old thinking his world was going to end. I would look back at him, as if blankly watching a sci-fi thriller portraying the aftermath of an atomic holocaust. I'd mend his wounds and pat his back to let him know he was loved. Even though chaos ensued regularly in our tiny apartment, we still managed to be each other's biggest supporter, teacher, and student.

Anthony was a tall, dark, and lanky man who possessed a fiery, Middle Eastern temper, and a never-satisfied air of French sophistication. He had specific names and occupations for everything in his home. Before I met him, the kitchen had never been used. He ran his tight ship with an iron fist and I, in turn, was the sea: choppy, unpredictable, and flood prone.

The day that Anthony and I first met was telling. I was supposed to have dinner with my parents who had recently come up from North Carolina for a rare mini vacation. This meant that my father had a work engagement in the city, and someone was paying for an extra night's stay at his hotel by the waterfront. My mother's consistent criticism was grating on my last nerve and I felt like I was being pulled back into an inescapable vortex of her misery. I left after waiting over an hour at the hotel for my older brother and father to get back from a baseball game and headed back to Brooklyn to spend quality time with my own four-legged child, whom I knew would never let me down.

When I got home, he was panting from the summer heat and jumping around with a toy in his mouth, happy to see me. I was living in Clinton Hill, which was about fifteen minutes from Fort Greene Park. It was dusk on the Fourth of July and I made my way out the door wearing a baseball cap, a red t-shirt and my long cargo shorts. I had just come back from Jamaica, so my style wasn't exactly New York chic.

During our walk, I noticed a tall pillar poking out of a line of trees directing me to the park. I was looking forward to watching the fireworks from our perfect vantage point above the buildings along Flatbush Avenue. When Charlie and I arrived, a quiet man with a funny hat was watching me from the concrete embankment near the monument. I was talking Patua to a Jamaican American family as their children rambunctiously teased Charlie.

Eventually, the man came up to us and asked if my dog was friendly, as if asking me on a date right then and there. I said, "Yes," and he proceeded to pet my dog without taking his eyes off me and trying to find something intelligent to say to me other than, "Hello." I thought he was the sweetest man I'd met in a good while, never knowing we would end up spending the next two and a half years of our lives with each other. We moved in together that month and never looked back.

He loved me and he loved my dog. And he didn't run away when I challenged him. He helped me learn how to stick around when things got tough and taught me all those big life lessons one usually learns growing up in a normal family. I cradled him when he needed comfort and made him homemade chicken soup when he got sick. I applied acne cream on his back, and he extracted blackheads from my nose. We loved each other and I was finding out what real intimacy was like.

Anthony was a very quiet, shy man who had a romantic, childlike quality about him, but also a dark and calculated side. It shifted in the later part of the first year, and he became a little more tightly wound the longer I knew him. Being a lot younger and still in the "everything I touch turns to shit" phase of my life, he felt obliged to kick my ass a few times to slowly force me to pick up the pieces. I started to gain a healthy confidence in myself due partly to his guidance, and partly to the new miracle drugs I was taking to handle my supposed depression. I began to understand much more about adulthood; something I'd been avoiding at all costs, because I just didn't have the foundations necessary to comprehend it.

Of course, my family loved him right off the bat. What wasn't to love? He was handsome, successful, and incredibly smart. But even then, things had to settle down before they could call him something other than my "friend." I had come out two years prior and made sure everyone was okay with that. I didn't care any more about holding back who I was for the sake of others because I had spent too much of my life doing so already.

I relished the idea of being able to hold his hand in front of my parents who had never really known anyone who was gay. I looked at it more as an opportunity to show the world and myself it's okay. So when things got tough with Anthony, I blamed myself because I didn't want to believe that our relationship was never meant to be forever.

When I first told my mom I was gay, she recoiled as she usually did whenever I found the courage to come to her with a personal problem. She moved around uncomfortably to sit a little more comfortable on her extra-large couch. Staring straight into my eyes, she said to me in a whisper, "You know you're going to have a sad, lonely life…don't you, Danny? I'm glad I didn't tell you it was okay to be gay because you would have been an even bigger whore than you already are now." The unfortunate part was not what she said, or how she said it; it was that I always felt that she never really knew me. Her response to this news just confirmed those suspicions.

My father, on the other hand, took it somewhat differently. He was in his office upstairs when I asked him to come into the bedroom as I finished ironing his dress shirts. I told him I had something to tell him that was important. He sat down with clenched buttocks expecting the worst.

"You know I'm gay, right?" He was shocked and started to break down in a defeated kind of pleading.

"It's all my fault, Danny."

Having to deal with what my mother had told me earlier and now what my father was going to say to somehow break the ice, I was unfortunately ready for anything. The gloves were off.

"Alright, Dad. Why is it your fault?"

"Well, when you got cancer, the doctors said that the medication they were going to give you might change your genes and make you gay. And your mother and I selfishly wanted to save your life and so…well, it's all my fault."

Taking in the profundity of what had just transpired, I suddenly thought to myself: *If this is the genetic make-up that I am biologically derived from, then I thank God I'm a flaming faggot!*

I waited for him to settle down before I said, "Alright, Dad. If that's what you believe, then that's your deal. But if you are interested in learning more about reality, I'll be downstairs making you an omelet!" With that, I was out the door leaving the iron on full heat.

When he finally came downstairs, I had already put the cheese and the ham in the eggs and was flipping them over in the skillet just like Julia Child taught me to do. Looking down at the pan, I braced myself for what type of rubbish might come out of his lips next. I could almost hear the wheels turning in his head and felt bad for the emaciated gerbil that was still stuck in his cage, hanging on for dear life.

"You know, Dan…I have this friend, Rudd, who has this beautiful daughter…"

I looked at him clear in the eyes, the way my mother always loved to do, and said, "If you want this omelet, you'll sit down and shut up! Your son's a homosexual! Get used to it!"

To which he replied, "All you need is a good, strong woman, Danny."

I retorted, "All I need is a dad and a mother with a little more compassion and understanding. Really, Dad…for a man with two doctorate degrees, you really are a jerk sometimes." I gathered my keys like I'd done a hundred times before and got into my Saturn, three-door coupe with the rainbow lei hanging from the rear-view mirror, started the engine, and peeled down the driveway in a contemptuous cloud of exhaust and pollen.

I always kept my clothes stuffed in a bag in the backseat just in case I had to make a quick getaway. It was a trick I learned on those many difficult nights growing up, when situations at home got to be too much for any human to handle. I would usually end up at the gym or at my first lover, Matt's, house for the night. I'd stay out, sometimes sleeping in K-Mart parking lots until the morning, when I'd realize I had no money for food and was late for school. I kept coming back home because I felt that as bad as it got, it could always be worse, and I had to help my parents learn just as much as I needed their help to struggle. This time, however, I decided I'd let them marinate in the unfortunate information they were just given about their son that they had such high, heterosexual hopes for.

As I rounded the bend of the highway towards Cary, I recalled the many nights I'd drive over to Matt's apartment. He lived with his family who were always so kind and accommodating, never outright knowing that he and I were secretly lovers. I was so very thankful I had the opportunity to leave my home when I needed to. I had few responsibilities back then that would leave me to fend for myself in a place that was surrounded by people who never understood me. It just made it that much harder when the people you cared for most couldn't love you the way you wanted them to.

It was almost dawn, and I was a couple of miles into Virginia when I popped in my favorite Jason Robert Browne CD. I smiled as I opened my mouth to sing, "A new world calls across the ocean…" It seemed fitting at the time. Listening to showtunes on cruise control as the sun came up over Richmond, I thought to myself, *how am I ever going to find a way to continue living like this?*

Bowling for Love in the Bumper Lanes

"Don't feed the hungry," Anthony said while we watched those telethon commercials on television, "Clothe the hungry!" My partner at the time's primary reason for living was to make skinny girls feel beautiful and fat girls contemplate suicide. His favorite meal was French-pressed coffee with a flaky, chocolate croissant from The Green Grape around the corner. It was as close to Paris as he was going to get in Brooklyn. The only problem was that this was usually his only meal of the day. "Who wants to be fat," he'd extol as we walked together down Fulton Avenue. I solemnly agreed, looking down to notice how my pants' button was about to pop off.

I'd slowly become a model for Anthony's outdated apparel; the clothes that reminded him fondly of the days before we met. Those were the days when he had money to spend on things he wanted; free to claw his way up the corporate ladder where fashion moguls basked in each other's sneers and crippling defeats. Now, he was left with two more mouths to feed and all the drama that came with being in a monogamous, gay relationship.

I did make our lives as comfortable as possible and took care of him as any good househusband could. I did the laundry, cooked the meals, and worked with him at the studio, so that Anthony could live a peacefully secluded life on the top floor of a tree-lined brownstone. I listened to him gripe about the business, I petted him when he needed attention, and gave him love the best I knew how to. It was a pleasant existence for a while and gave me the opportunity to recall the times when I didn't have it so well. Anthony would scathingly remind me of this every time we disagreed on subjects like clothing or the physical consumption of calories.

A year before I met him, I was living on the West Side and about to turn 27. My roommate was a middle-aged, gay lawyer who had devoured more books than anyone I've ever known. There were black and white photos of past lovers and budding flowers in thin, gray frames. His couch could swallow you whole and his kitchen was the cutest nook I'd ever seen.

His bathroom had all original Pepto-Bismol pink subway tiles, and all his products were stationed about in sturdy lines of obsessive compulsion. His books, which were the predominant focal point of his one-bedroom flat, were stacked up in the apartment, partitioning my makeshift bedroom from the living room. At the time, it worked quite well, seeing as how I had nothing else to call my own.

One morning I woke up to find a water bug that I mistook for a giant cockroach crawling on my face; the difference between the two, I've yet to fully decipher. I did the only thing my instincts would allow me to do. I punched myself in the face a couple of times and the bug finally fell off, scurrying across my white Egyptian cotton sheets. I ran to Bill's room screaming like a banshee. He answered half-asleep, ready to murder any intruder that he happened to encounter.

The only thing about what happened that took me for a loop was that he was completely naked and that for such a short man, he had the largest penis I'd seen in a very long time. Granted, it was the only penis I'd seen in over a year, but it was impressive to say the least, and led me to seriously reconsider the idea of relative size.

At that time, I was working at a huge outlet space in midtown that housed sample sales and retail stores that were desperate to sell and were usually going out of business. All the while, I was substitute teaching whenever someone needed a young, expendable arts instructor. After babysitting spawns from Hell that sucked every joyous wish their parents once had, I swore that every class would soon be my last. Then I'd get a call out of the blue with someone on the other line in dire straits, and I would show up on time, thinking that I was saving the lives of every student I met. Turns out, the only thing I eventually saved by not answering my phone each morning was my sanity.

I was still auditioning for performing gigs here and there, and life as a performer was becoming less and less enjoyable. What was first the most exciting career, quickly turned out to be a grueling, arduous, freak show; one that I'd meant to cancel my subscription to on several occasions. I had reached the pinnacle of my marketable youth and had only heartache to show for it. I decided something needed to change and I didn't want to wait for success to find me any longer.

I began toying with the idea of online dating as a way of making life a little less awkward. I talked the idea over with my roommate, Bill, and he offered seasoned advice as best he could.

"Isn't it dangerous?" I asked.

"No way, everyone does it. They just don't want to admit it, you see. Look…"

Instead of quelling my fears by helping me find an appropriate dating site that would accept IOUs in exchange for monthly subscription fees, he showed me his profile on manhunt.com, asking me if I had any peculiar fetishes I'd be interested in pursuing. After staring at thumbnails of naked men with blurred faces, I thanked him begrudgingly and turned toward the kitchen to hang my head in a lukewarm cup of chamomile.

I was on three sites at one time, which I thought in the beginning was the perfect idea, because it increased my chances of finding Mr. Right right now. The only problem was that it multiplied my chances exponentially of being contacted by the craziest people I've ever met in my life.

The first date I went on, I got to the coffee shop a little early to make sure the coast was clear, in case I needed to make a quick getaway. I tested all the emergency exits and gave nearby patrons my safeword in case I needed them to call the authorities. I went ahead and ordered my chai latte so that I could secretly analyze the man's character from a safe vantage point, while he was undoubtedly in line buying a double espresso.

A very large man, almost 7 feet tall and weighing close to 250 pounds came in through the front doors reminding me much of "Stewart" from the TV show, *MadTV*. He was wearing a short, tight shirt, and sported a permanent facial expression reminiscent of a confused Mormon. When he came into the light, I noticed his worry lines were framed by a thick bowl cut, and his glasses glistened atop a few overactive sebatious glands.

He sat down with a giggle of excitement and said, "You must be Dan?"

Befuddled, I answered, "Yes, and you are?"

"Oh, I Googled you after you responded to my ad on chemistry.com. I didn't know you were on Myspace?"

"Yes. I have a…listen, who are…"

He sat down in midsentence. "OMG, did you really travel around the country as an activist? I mean I read something about you were some sort of an activist and in some newspapers, in like Kansas or Seattle or something. I mean, God…that must have been hard talking to all those people and having to listen to…"

"I'm sorry. I didn't catch your name."

He covered his face in embarrassment. He used his neck muscles to push his head back and with a frightening grin he exposed rows of neck skin that made his head look like a giant penis.

"OMG. I'm sorry. I'm Mitchell. I'm your date! Yeeey!" (Insert insane laughter). He proceeded to clench his jaw and show every tooth in his mouth as if I was his dentist going in for a root canal on one of his back molars.

I decided to skip the whole relationship thing and just settled with crazy. "Yes, Mitchell. Of course. Hi. I'm sorry. You know, I've been thinking. We're just too different people. We're growing apart and it's just not working out between us anymore. Don't worry. It's not you…it's me."

"Oh, okay. Well, did you want to get some ice cream or, um…?

"Yeah. No. I'm sorry. Thank you."

"…I know this great place on..."

"No, Mitchell." I rested my palm on the top of his trembling right hand. His clammy skin felt loose, like wet paper mâché.

"Please. Let me go. This is harder for me than it is for you. I have to go now, Mitchell." I touched his quivering lip with every fingerprint I had on my left index finger before he had a chance to speak.

"This is the best for both of us. Trust me. Goodbye, Mitchell."

I gave my best soap opera exit, making sure I still had one eye on the crazy before I checked every pocket for my wallet and apartment keys. Just like that, our five-minute whirlwind of a relationship came to an abrupt and appreciated end.

I crossed the street and observed the overgrown manchild sip a strawberry milkshake through a thick straw, wiping whipped cream and snot on the sleeve of his extra-small hoodie. With tears dropping onto his frosted loaf of organic carrot cake, I watched from a distance as the dramatic scene unfolded. Standing there on the corner of 49th and Broadway, I felt so sorry for Mitchell and horrified at the thought of who else I would encounter along this treacherous terrain toward love.

My second adventure in the online world of dating was with an actor named Fernando. He was a 5′5 Latin man who had a very caring face. He detested cartoons and comic books, so I thought it was an appropriate start from where I was only days prior. Scarred by my previous experience, I went with the complete opposite and prayed he wasn't secretly wearing *Sesame Street* underwear.

We met at a movie theatre in Chelsea to see the movie *Juno*. It had just come out and sounded like a great date flick. Something that could make you find a pregnant teen protagonist relatable, yet was twisted enough to offer palpable, subtle wit, was always a winner in my book. I arrived early to purchase my ticket, which was the usual technique I employed to thwart any issues at the box office while courting disaster.

Fernando arrived on time and gave me a great, big hug with open arms. I found it endearing, so I didn't close my eyes all the way. I proceeded to lightly pat him on his back with my right hand. It was surprisingly nice to see a clear view of the Empire State Building over the top of his head.

The whole time we were watching the film he was staring longingly into the side of my skull. It freaked me out and eventually I couldn't stand it any longer. I turned toward him and said, "What? What? Do I have something in my ear or something? What are you staring at?"

He answered me passionately saying, "You are so beautiful. I think you are amazing!"

I sank down into my seat and apologized for my rude behavior. After that thwarted kerfuffle, we couldn't take our hands off each other. He made me feel so desired at a time when I felt so alone and utterly useless. It was the first time anyone had ever said those two sentences to me; at least one after the other and not followed with a, "Psych" or an "I'm just kidding!" I was a kid in a candy store and couldn't wait to unwrap my just deserts.

I was intoxicated by his fondness for me, but when he asked if I wanted to listen to "Liza With A Z" at his apartment in Queens, I hesitated for a moment. I knowingly avoided Queens like the clap, but I really wanted to see who Fernando was in private. We got to his apartment and I did my best to play the good girl. He handed me a glass of wine in a paper cup and a couple of chocolate eggs he had left over from Easter. At least he was Catholic and wouldn't try anything frisky until after the third date.

And just like that, he was on top of me. He ripped off my black, short-sleeved, dress shirt (the one I only wore when I wanted to look mysterious or coquettishly unavailable) and started biting me on my chest. Like a rabid jackrabbit, he began to furiously hump my leg, as I pushed on his shoulder and hip to come up for air. At the scene of the crime was an old, yard-sale couch that was hideous to look at but oddly comfortable to be tussled upon for the moment.

Fernando looked at me with his eyes burning, unbuttoning his belt with his tiny, stubby fingers. Rubbing up against me with long, thrusting intervals, I could smell his spicy cologne and natural Latin body odor that sadly reminded me of my father. I looked away and started to imagine Carey Elwes from *The Princess Bride*. "As. You. Wish." I muttered from beneath his pelvic thrusts.

Fernando started whispering in my ear and the perfect make-out session I was having with Elwes turned into a threesome with Inigo Montoya. I remembered my DARE classes in elementary school and just said, "No, no, NO!"

I looked around the room to make sure there were no hidden cameras or crucifixes on display. I hardly had time to admire his Impressionist print of a country farmhouse and the way his framed *Cabaret* playbill signed by Allan Cummings was tilted to the right on that one fiery-orange, painted wall. I moved my head to side to get some air and he grabbed my face and turned it toward the back of the couch and proceeded to bite and suck the side of my neck. Confused and breathing into the smoke-ridden fibers of his loveseat, I finally found the strength to push him off me. Fernando landed on the floor with a soft, tiny thud.

Like a jack-in-the-box, he sprang back into action. I landed back on the couch, and this time wished I had thought about buying one of those pocket-sized cans of pepper spray. I strategically thrusted my left knee up into his swollen crotch. He gasped and coughed with startled eyes. I raced to the door after grabbing my keys off the *I Love Lucy* memorabilia ashtray. He scraped for a fistful of my clothing with his nails, barely missing my pant leg by a fraction of an inch. Huddled in a corner of the room, he tightly held his groin, as I struggled with the deadbolt. But it wouldn't budge.

Fernando, seeing his prey fleeing the scene of the crime, crawled his way to the door. I jiggled the handle and kicked the bottom of the door with my Asics. Whining and falling down the stairs toward the front door like something out of a *Poltergeist* movie, he grabbed onto my shirt and pulled with all his weight. I screamed bloody murder as the door finally swung open. I ran to the subway praying to God his dick wouldn't regain consciousness. The subway doors closed, and I watched Queens leave my sight.

Given the fiasco with Mitchell, the overgrown Peter Pan, and Fernando the pocket-sized nympho, I decided to cool off on the whole online dating thing for a while. That lasted about 24 hours--until I was contacted by a man named Edward.

Edward was a dancer. He had his master's degree and was slightly taller than me with blonde hair. From the extensive research I conducted into his online profile, he looked very promising, and exuded the kind of sexy charm only an intelligent dancer could. I answered his message, and we began to correspond on a regular basis. Every day at work I couldn't think of anything other than opening my email that night to see what cute things Edward had written to me.

He didn't say very much. In fact, his responses were usually three lines at best. Normally, this would have pissed me off, but I welcomed the silent type for the time being.

We decided to meet up at the 72nd street entrance of Central Park around 4 p.m. Unfortunately, I arrived on time to find Edward already waiting by the hotdog stand. He met me with a handshake and a nod of his head. I instantly fell in love with his normal, relaxed demeanor.

At the time, I was working at a fancy French restaurant in midtown and was making good money for the first time in my life. I could afford to take Edward out on a few occasions, which made me happy. We went to my favorite vegan place, Candle 79, and ordered a bottle of wine. I felt very adult and giddy with excitement to actually be dating a man as gorgeous and mysterious as Edward.

Of course, my luck would run out when he started realizing that I was way too head-over-heels for him. I started making dates in my mind of where we were going to meet and making reservations without remembering to tell him. When he said, "I'll talk to you later," I instantly bought two tickets to see *Chicago* and was devastated when he didn't show up at will call. We communicated via text and my bill started climbing into triple digits, which was not a pattern of behavior I was capable of continuing. I got the hint the day he took his profile off the website and moved back to the Midwest.

I couldn't figure out exactly what went wrong until I watched a news story of a crazed stalker who attacked an actress downtown. I glanced up from my computer screen, overheating from exhaustion, and noticed the number of messages I had left on my dating site inbox. What was once a full and overflowing cornucopia of possibilities, was now down to two unread reminders from headquarters telling me renew my membership or lose my account access. I remembered being the new guy in town when all the other hunks with screennames without faces like "RoughRider" and "BackDoorBoy" were lining up to compete for a date with moi. They used to send me winks as superficial tokens of their cyberlust. Now I was back at square-one wondering where I went wrong.

One man did end up contacting me. His name was named Jim. He lived in Hoboken. His profile described his love of tattoos and leather, and his picture displayed something to the effect of bare genitalia adorned with a slew of shiny chains and piercings. I cancelled my memberships and threw my face into the pillow for a cold, hard cry.

Defeated and frustrated, I told Bill I was going to kill myself or die a lonely old man. He looked at me with a mouthful of Ben and Jerry's and said, "Come on. There's someone I want you to meet. Now, he's a little older than you, but he doesn't seem to mind that kind of thing. He lives in Hoboken and I found him on Manhunt.com. His name is Jim, and I've been talking with him for about a week or so. He seems really hot! You interested?"

I graced the wall with my eyes and took a deep, sorrowful breath. "No, Bill. Sadly, this meat's off the market until further notice."

"Check, Please!"

Bringing Anthony to a Jewish seder was like taking Hitler to see a Mel Brooks musical. You have no idea what to expect if the brisket is bad or what to do when the laughs eventually die down. Like a giant metronome, my eyes scanned the room from one side of the table to the other, saying a little prayer in the back of my borrowed yamaka that we would all make it out of there alive.

Luckily the dinner was divine, not counting the awkward moment when our host mistook Elijah's sacred cup for his fifth glass of Manischewitz, or when the dinner conversation gradually turned to opinions on the current health care debate. It was then that I began to rock back and forth in my chair, tapping out my last will and testament under the table in Morse code, praying I wouldn't have to hold Anthony's tongue for much longer. Astoundingly, the effects of kosher wine kept the beast at bay until we were safely home alone.

I hadn't seen Michelle since we were in Jamaica, and the last time I remember seeing her husband, Oded, we were both stoned out of our gourds on the patio of his hotel room at the Ritz. Fifteen minutes into him explaining his perspective on spirituality, I gathered what little wits I had left, propped my head up from its reclined position and sputtered, "Honey…you lost me at 'Hadassah!'" I then got up from the lounge chair and ran directly into the sliding glass doors, having mistaken them for rainbows.

Michelle and I had both worked for Fitbodies, Inc. and met in Jamaica. She was a petite Black, consumer lawyer, who lived in Park Slope and could kick the shit out of me if she really wanted to. I was already there at the resort when Michelle came in for the week to teach classes. Oded and their son, Jaden, arrived days later. Oded was a tall middle eastern man with a handsome bald head and an "MD" attached to his name. He left half-way through the seder to look at x-rays of impacted colons.

In Jamaica, I took Michelle through the usual routines and we sat in on each other's classes for support. We bonded and began to have a budding "gaymance." This is when a gay man and a straight woman bond so closely that everyone around them would swear they were a couple, thus allowing either party to be more socially accepted. If you were having a gaymance with a beautiful woman, you were okay to be gay in Jamaica. So I was considered the luckiest White guy on the island for several months, as each traveling fitness professional made her way through my door. Everyone there just assumed that I was straight, but with a little extra sugar in my tank.

The first time I entered Michelle's master suite, I realized how foolish I was to have considered my garden-view hotel room the ultimate pied-a-terre. Jaden had been constipated since they landed, and as if he was one of my students, I knelt to show him a yoga pose that would help move fecal matter through his intestines quickly and efficiently. He jumped out of his mother's arms, smacked me on the back after calling me "butthead," and ran away before I could say "child's pose."

I wondered how Jaden would receive Anthony and I at the seder since I was bringing over a man who undoubtedly looked like a praying mantis had mated with an owl. *What was going to come out of his mouth during the exodus from Egypt? Would he call me out at dinner when remembering our initial encounter?* Thankfully no. He had forgotten all about our little misunderstanding and looked at me as if I was just another schmuck he would have to deal with for the next couple of hours.

As the Passover celebration ended, Anthony graciously thanked our hosts and pushed his chair back into the table. Sloshed and sporting one of Michelle's dark, curly wigs, I managed to make it into their private elevator. Before leaving, Michelle gave me a goodbye kiss, as Oded whizzed by us clinging to a picture of a woman's ovaries. Before the elevator doors closed, Jaden came riding by on his fancy red tricycle, as both parents were discussing legalities in the back hallway. He waved his hands to the departing guests, then stopped and stood halfway upright, one hand still on his prized possession. He looked at me and repeated, as innocently as ever, "Bye-bye, Butthead! Bye-Bye, Butthead!" The doors couldn't have closed fast enough.

A Puerto Rican Dis-Easter

Anthony and I decided to visit my relatives in New Jersey for a well-deserved Easter vacation with Charlie. Since I hadn't learned from our Passover experience to lay low during the Holy holidays, I thought this would be a great way to get out of the city for a change.

Grandma was living with my aunt while her home on Bronxdale Avenue was being fumigated to sell in a hostile market. She had had a breakdown a few months prior, was treated at a mental hospital, and later released. It was going to be strange seeing grandma in the daylight.

She had been prepped before we arrived that Anthony was more than "just a friend." It took her a couple of days to get over the initial shock that almost half of her grandchildren were card-carrying members of the pink team. Still, her reaction to Anthony, who arrived decked out in Martin Margiela, was pleasantly welcoming as compared to the time Nicole brought home a Black man.

"Why you no get noady mas mehor? Dees Blek mang ees no bueno!"

She couldn't see the fact that he had a college degree, a good job, and was a very sweet man. She maintained that Nicole wouldn't be able to see anything but his teeth when they had sex and would eventually lose him if there were a blackout at home. She had this amazing ability to degrade people while protesting she was only trying to help.

Upon our arrival, we were showered with rice and beans, as my cousins came to hug me and greet my first real boyfriend. They were so happy to see us. It didn't take long until the dinner conversation turned to "Danny's Most Embarrassing Moments in Recent History." I was never, for example, going to live down the time when I was thirteen and asked my titi for help with a very delicate, personal matter.

"It burns, titi!"

"What did you do to it, Danny?"

"I don't know. I was in the bathroom for like an hour and when I came out it started hurting."

"What were you doing in the bathroom?"

"Nothing. Umm…why?"

"Let me take a look."

Not only did I have to expose the "hose beast" to my godmother the doctor, I had to also explain why my penis was bent and bright red. There was just no other option at the time given the fact that I couldn't walk without severe pain, and Titi was the only person I knew who had her own in-home pharmaceutical storage facility.

"Jesus Christ, Danny! What did you do?"

I started to cry, thinking that I permanently lost my chances to experience sex with a human being and that I was going to walk that way for ever. My future career as a back-up dancer for Janet Jackson was over, and I would have to dance at my eighth-grade prom in a full body cast.

"Come with me."

She took me by the arm to the bathroom with a packet of ointment in her hand and told me to apply it on the exterior ridge between my glans and corpora cavernosa. I was to only to use enough to cover the area and nothing more, and to refrain from rubbing or touching it for any extended period. I stood there with my pants down around my ankles, a packet of burn cream in one hand, and my broken penis in the other watching my aunt leave the room trying not to laugh.

"And Danny…use a lubricant next time."

Anthony covered his mouth and tried not to imagine me in the bathroom stall of a Wendy's yanking my pubescent schlong for a little under an hour. I had almost started a fire and had no idea that my first experience masturbating wasn't supposed to be so devastatingly painful. From that day forward, I was going to rethink the concept of "tug of war" and apply generously before rubbing vigorously.

As if that wasn't horrible enough, my cousins also discussed the time I was hit by a taxi just for the amusement of present company.

"Hey, Danny? Weren't you hit by a taxi?"

"Yes, Andrea. Thank you for reminding me."

"How far did you fly again?"

"About twenty feet. My shoe popped off and everything. You happy now?"

The whole family was in an uproar and forced me to reenact the entire ordeal for their listening and viewing pleasure. With my head held low, I proceeded to interpretively dance the events that had transpired on that fateful day. I turned my head to look both ways, as if crossing a busy intersection. Taking one step off the imaginary curb, I smacked my hands together and yelled "Bam!" I mimed flying through the air, tumbling onto the hard concrete, and dizzily getting back up again, brushing bits of glass and pavement off my clothes. They all sat there with their eyes glued to my every movement, holding their stomachs in riotous laughter. Then, I pointed my index finger into the air and turned it around in a circle, miming an ambulance siren that was fast approaching.

"How are you feeling, Sir?"

"Oh, I just got hit by a car. How are you?"

"Don't turn your head, but you just demolished a taxi and half of it is in pieces down Park Avenue."

"Thank you for alerting me. How's my hair?"

After gorging ourselves on the rest of our pollo guisado, the conversation turned to remembering grandpa who had died a couple of years back. We checked to see if grandma was in the kitchen, but we heard telenovelas blasting from Steven's old room, so we didn't bother to keep our mouths shut.

Both of my grandfathers fought in World War II; one was a prisoner of war and one was a secretary. My paternal grandpa was Puerto Rican and used to make up stories of flying warplanes through enemy territory while blowing up Nazi headquarters with grenades and handheld missiles. It turns out that he was stationed behind a desk in the safety of an American military base, typing letters, and sealing envelopes. After the war, he took a few jobs to get by and ended up working for the post office until he retired. My maternal grandfather was mostly Germanic and never talked about the war. Instead, he taught me how to knee slap "Camptown Races" and tap the Morse code on the bathroom wall with the back of a spoon.

My Puerto Rican grandpa, Miguel, the retired letter carrier, was a short, plump, bald man, who used to scare his grandkids by pulling the excess skin on his eyelids out to a protruding point and growling like an angry dog. His wife, Aida, used to pull out her dentures and hold them in front of our faces while we screamed bloody murder.

Miguel was confined to the basement of the Bronxdale Avenue house while Aida took the two remaining floors and all the air-conditioning that came with it. For dinner, we saw grandma standing in front of the stove eating bread and drinking Diet Pepsi. We would smell the delicious cooking and never knew where it was coming from. My little brother and I thought she was performing magic and that inside a box of Sazon were little packets of fairy dust.

We would hear footsteps and grandma would walk around the corner out of sight. Then we heard yelling, a door slam shut, and what sounded like a large bag of books falling down the stairs. Just like that, our dinner appeared, and was served by my grandmother with an evil smirk on her face. We would tell her how delicious the food was, as she finished the rest of her soda and huffed by the darkened kitchen sink.

Grandma led us all to believe that grandpa was always sleeping. But upon further investigation, I realized that what I was told for so long was not even remotely true. I snuck down the stairs to his stale-smelling lair, past the noisy water heater and to the right of an old painting depicting a man praying over a loaf of bread and a bowl of soup. Beyond the cheap planks of wood-paneling nailed to the walls, I witnessed grandpa holding his left arm up to the heavens and pulling it back to his heart as he recited an old Spanish love poem. In the silence, as if he had an imaginary spotlight on his chubby, wrinkled face, he would recount the details of his lover's hair and how passionately she inspired his soul to breathe.

Walking toward him, I called his name a few times without any response. I touched his shoulder to bring him out of the trance and he looked back at me after clearing his throat.

"Danito, que lindo, how are you?"

"I'm fine, Grandpa, how are you?"

"Oh, you know. I'm thankful to be alive. How's your Grandma?"

"She's fine."

"Good. That's good."

The Breakup

It was supposed to be less messy, but the inevitable breakup between Anthony and I was the toughest thing I had to let go of. For the past year and a half things were going downhill and it was clear that a breakup was fast approaching.

Anthony was working out a lot and taking some hefty supplements, while I was trying to finish up grad school in one piece. He was getting hornier, and I was getting more and more turned off because I just wasn't interested like I once was. He wanted more from me than I was able to give him, and it finally became too much for us both.

A relationship that was built on deep love and support for one another was turning into physical fights and verbal abuse. Our arguments had never been easy and became battles that lasted well into the morning. I'd beg him to let me sleep in a corner of the living room, so that I could wake up in a few hours to carry out another eighteen-hour day. But it was never enough, and Charlie was unfortunately always used as bait. I was living in a hell that I never thought I'd be in. For someone who was so good at leaving, I found myself enduring agonizing, sleepless nights because I didn't think I deserved any better.

It was quite a complicated situation, because both of us were trying to make the other person understand our side. I learned that the harder one pressed, the less appealing having a side became. I was never interested in persuading someone to change, and I thought that I'd be able to mature enough to eventually get to his level. I was under the false impression that relationships of magnitude could be handled much more civilly. When it became clear that the fights had little to do with what was going on and more to do with our own deep-seeded personal issues, the less I wanted to continue what I felt was irrational argumentation and abuse.

My requests for solitude prompted vitriol and his demands for my attention became impossible to fulfill. It was a never-ending cycle of madness that was only getting worse, and no bouquets of flowers sent to my work would make up for it. I never wanted flowers, or apologies, or promises, I only wanted peace for the both of us.

The night it all ended I had come home from work and found Anthony had consulted a spiritual advisor who told him that I was going to leave him. Not wanting this to happen he became much more menacing about controlling my every move. He began to put restrictions on how I was to refer to myself and what I was supposed to wear in public, who I could be friends with, and what types of television programming and reading material I was not allowed to consume. What had begun as an opportunity to learn from a man much older and wiser than I, became a cycle of coercion that no longer fit the man that I was becoming.

It seemed like I had nothing of value before I met him. Anthony molded me into a man who successfully completed graduate school, held down two respectable jobs, and founded two student organizations on campus. My drive and his support allowed me to accomplish a great many things that I may not have otherwise. However, I found myself getting involved in activities just to prove that I was "worthy" of his encouragement. Even though his behavior was aggressively manipulative, there was not an ounce of me that thought he did it for any other reason than because he loved and believed in me. I just wasn't the kind of person who wanted to have a relationship with someone who didn't know how to demonstrate love in a more relaxed and convivial manner.

So much of what I felt where his motivations stemmed from his lack of familial support. When Anthony came out in college, his father threatened his life and his mother did nothing to stop it. He moved to France, with nothing but the clothes on his back, and learned patternmaking from one of the finest fashion designers in Paris. He was intimately knowledgeable about hardship and when he moved back to the States to begin his fashion career, he realized how hard one needed to be in order to succeed in that industry. He was a truly ruthless, calculating, and brilliant individual. He had my respect, but I could not give him all my heart.

The night everything ended was indescribably painful. There wasn't a part of me that was not broken or scared then, and it took everything I had to get out of their alive.

I sat on the Capelinni, finishing some work on the computer when Anthony walked into the bedroom, closed the door and windows, and asked me one burning question. I knew something was up but was not prepared for what would transpire.

He seemed a bit desperate. I could tell he had been thinking about how he was going to broach the subject with me for a while.

"I don't want you to see that girl again?"

"What girl, Anthony?"

"That girl, Ashley. She's no good for you."

I was taken aback by his accusations that my friend, Ashley, was somehow bad for me. And instead of questioning him, which would have led to more heartache, I simply said, "lease stop talking about Ashley. If there's something you want to talk about that is between you and me, then that's fine. But Ashley has nothing to do with this."

He railed into me, demanding I never speak to her again, that she was going to rip us apart and it would all be my fault. He shouted, clenching his fists and yelled, "I said, no! You're never going to see her again!"

I tried to leave the room on several attempts, but he blocked the doorway every time. I was feeling panicky, but was trying to contain myself, to say the right things, and to plan what I would do in case things continued to escalate. All the while, he looked into my eyes with fear, desperation, and grave satisfaction. He held my arms, as I did my best to rip myself out of his grip. He tracked me across the wall with his taunts as I tried to make sense of it all.

"Why are you doing this? Please stop. Let me go."

I had had enough of the fights, of feeling manipulated and fearful of saying the wrong thing or wearing the wrong thing. I tried to leave and he kept pushing and pulling me back to where he was in the room. I knew it wasn't going to end well. And so it began.

He pulled me onto the Capellini. I got on top and tried to hold him down saying, "Stop! Stop! Stop!" He would only repeat, "No! No! No!" Our grips turned to kicks and eventually there was no stopping the train wreck. I felt caged with no one there to help me. I was stuck and starving for air, and I had to think quickly to get the hell out.

I ran to the window and opened it and yelled outside for someone to call the cops. An onlooker saw me and stopped. Anthony pushed me away and said, "Nothing to see here. Everything's fine." But it wasn't, not by a long shot.

I ran inside for my phone that was on the living room table. He grabbed the cell phone out of my hands and broke it into pieces, smashing it several times on the glass corner of the patternmaking table. I watched him try to break my wrist with his two bare hands as my eyes widened not believing what was happening. I banged on the walls for a neighbor to help. I ran to the door and yelled out into the hallway for someone--anyone who was within earshot--but no one came. Anthony pulled me back and continued his rampage. Charlie hid under the table beside himself in fear. I couldn't blame him.

I was already shaking and exhausted from fending for my life. I ran to the landline to call 911. He pulled it out of my hands and smashed it into a million pieces on the hardwood floor. Regardless of whether it made sense, the only thing I knew to do was to find a way to get out of there, or I was going to die. It felt as simple as that.

I ran toward the bathroom, the only other door that had a lock in the apartment. I got in, but he tried to keep me from locking the door by pulling it open and turning the knobs. I somehow was able to secure the lock at just the right time, and Anthony continued banging furiously. The lock wasn't holding completely, and he had found a way to pull the door open. There was nothing else I could do, and no one was coming to my aid. I grabbed a bottle of laundry detergent that was by the toilet. The moment Anthony got inside the room and went for me, he got a huge slug of the detergent bottle across his face. He lunged for my neck and I literally fought for my life.

I finally ran back into the bedroom where all my stuff was. I had made up my mind to leave him for good right then and there and I threw on my clothes as fast as possible. He headed toward my computer to break it because he knew that was the only thing I had left that was helping me create a better life for myself. Knowing how much of my writings and collegiate career was in that contraption--before the days of cloud-based storage and automatic backups--I fought to hold it close to my chest.

I saw the moment when he had reached his last option. His age was showing now, and he was almost completely out of breath. The onlookers outside had amassed a small posse and were all yelling at me to get out and that they had just called the police.

I grabbed a small bag, my computer, and left wearing only my tank top, shorts and sandals. The fight had lasted a good half an hour or so and my eyes were bloodshot from crying. My voice was hoarse from screaming and I had bruises and cuts along my neck, face, and arms.

The first place I could go to where I thought he wouldn't find me was the dance studio a few blocks away. I had been taking classes at the studio and it was the only place that I knew would be open at that time of the night.

When I arrived, I noticed they were close to closing, so I walked in as inconspicuously as possible. I asked to use the phone, but I had no way of calling anyone as my phone was lying in a million pieces on Anthony's floor. The guy behind the counter knew something was up and had seen me there before so he knew I wasn't completely crazy. I pulled out my laptop and it powered up. I connected to the wifi in the building and went on Facebook to see if any of my friends were online. I contacted my friend Ruba, asked her to contact Ashley for me, gave her the number of the studio to call, and said that it was an emergency. When Ashley called, I instantly knew that I'd be okay.

It was the closest I had felt to freedom in a long time. I met Ashley at her apartment, and she gently nursed me back to health. I called my parents on her cell phone and got ahold of my mother.

Her first words were, "Danny? What did you do? What did you do?"

Shocked, I asked what she was talking about, and she whispered in the most serious and assuming tone, "I know what you did. Anthony told us everything."

I responded that I didn't have time to defend what had just transpired and that if she truly cared about her son, she would have asked me how I was, rather than assuming I was somehow at fault.

She then said, "Is that a threat?"

My not understanding where she was coming from and her inability to see the situation any other way than how she assumed it went down based upon her affinity for distrust left me with little options. I waited for her to say something to me that would help me make sense of the situation, instead I was met with even more ugly, presumptive, attacks. I told her that I would speak to her at a time that was more convenient for both of us, that I had just experienced something very traumatic and that I needed to find a way to take care of myself.

Ashley heard the whole conversation on speakerphone and was dumbfounded by my mother's reaction. I told her that it was par for the course for my fucked-up family and not to worry. I was safe with her for now. We planned to go back the next morning and I used Ashley's cell phone to text Anthony to arrange a time when I could take Charlie since I was pretty sure Anthony would try and use him as bait to keep me there.

The next morning Ashley and I went to the apartment. I walked in with one goal in mind: get Charlie, get work clothes, and get the hell out of there. I was met by Anthony wearing oversized sunglasses and his friend, Dawn, who was trying to find the right words to say. I walked out with everything I needed and that was the last time I ever saw Anthony again.

The next few weeks I continued work as usual trying to hide my physical wounds and inner turmoil. Anthony tried to contact me hundreds of times via email and social media. He was not only possessive, but unbelievably persistent. I could not allow myself to fall victim to his persuasion again. It had happened too many times before and I had to draw the line. I don't remember his last question to me, but my last response was, "I have already forgiven you. Please forgive me. It is over. Please let me go." He finally understood, or so I hoped.

I worked with the police to obtain the rest of my items, but Anthony refused to open the door for them when they showed up, even blowing out the candle he had burning in his bedroom window. *How French,* I thought. I then asked my friend, Athena, who was in contact with him to please help me get my things. She didn't understand the gravity of the situation and may have assumed I was just being dramatic.

I had to get a new phone and change all my contact information, because I was so afraid that Anthony was going to contact me again. Although it seemed harsh, I also had to distance myself from anyone who knew him, because Anthony was much smarter than I was, and I didn't put it past him to try and use his friends to get to me.

Charlie and I slept on a few couches over the weeks. I announced to my boss at work that I was moving to California. No one knew why, besides the fact that it was going to be a fresh start for me. I had finally received my graduate degree and I was turning thirty in a few weeks. I was finally on my own. As I prepared for my future move, I tried one last attempt to contact my parents. My mother had called my uncle to let him know what she believed happened. This was an unbelievably hurtful thing, but nothing out of the ordinary for my mother.

Throughout my life, my mother always assumed I was at fault for everything because when I was a child, I told her something that was happening to me that she never wanted to believe. I confided in her something that was occurring in our home that she was not aware of and did not want to investigate. I was a child when I told her on two separate occasions and from that point on, I was considered filth in her eyes. I found out weeks later that Anthony had told them the truth, but my mother had already made up her mind and chose to get other family members involved to bolster her twisted opinion of me.

Anthony's story was surprisingly spot on! He owned up to what he had done, but also admitted his actions stemmed from a desperate need to hold on to me. However, my mother was incapable of adequately mothering me, so understanding complex emotions was not a feasible endeavor. She'd been through enough stressful situations to learn how to deflect emotion and to direct blame where it suited her best. She jumped straight to nurse-mode and tried to mitigate anything that could lead to what she considered to be devastating consequences like jail or death. Psychological health, physical abuse, and emotional neglect were the least of her concerns.

I was in a nice quiet back hallway of the Rubin museum on a Sunday afternoon with Ashley, and I had requested my parents take a phone call from me at a specific time that day. I hoped the call would help us all gain clarity and allow my mother and I to reconcile our differences, giving us both the opportunity to see where the other was coming from. But like most of my dreams and wishes of familial rectification, this too was not going to turn out the way I had hoped.

They answered the call from two sides of the house: my mom from the downstairs line and my father in his office. I opened the conversation with gratitude and an explanation of the events that had transpired. My parents listened to me in complete silence, which I thought was a representation of their willingness to hear both sides, but I was dead wrong. It was the first time I'd ever experienced them that quiet.

When I was finished my mother said, "We already knew that. Anthony told us all of that already." Not only was that the first time I was hearing about this, but the fact that he had corroborated everything I said, and my mother was still giving me the third degree completely floored me. I asked why she reacted when I first called as if I was somehow at fault and she responded that I threatened her. I said that I'd never done that, nor was I in any space at the time to threaten anyone from whom I was seeking assistance, especially with witnesses around. Her assumptions got the better of her and I asked why she had contacted my family members to spread lies about me when the only thing I needed from her at the time was support. She then responded that she was trying to keep me from going to jail.

"Mom, then have the cops call me. I literally have nothing to hide. I did nothing wrong, I defended myself. I have pictures. I've told you before he was getting more physical with me and you didn't care then. What more do you want from me?"

Then, my dad chimed in at the worst possible moment as he seemed to do so well, telling me that Anthony was the best man I would ever find and that it was my fault things ended the way they did. "You should have learned how to keep your mouth shut!"

My father had a hard enough time understanding that two men could have a loving relationship and believed that if there was a fight, my mouth was likely to blame. After defending Anthony's actions, and how he saw the situation in his mind, my dad said, "You need to recognize who loves you in the world."

I had heard everything I needed to. I was dealing with two people who long ago had very high hopes for their "perfect" son before he "turned gay." But somewhere between being the good kid and narrowly escaping a pattern of domestic violence, I had somehow destroyed their version of who I was supposed to be for them. I was the kid who made everyone laugh (often at my own expense) and because I sought help for my own issues, I was making the biggest mistake of my life by leaving "a good thing."

My father's final words were "You'll never do any better than him in your life, Danny."

I could see that the heartfelt conversation I was hoping for was not even a remote possibility, so I told them they wouldn't have to worry about me any longer. There had been far too many hurtful things said, assumed, and done over the years, and I just couldn't see any of it getting any better with them any time soon. Then, my mother responded that she was tired of being verbally attacked. Stunned and perplexed, I rested my case. I couldn't play the victim game with her any longer. So, I said, "I love you, but you won't have to deal with me anymore. I've gotta go. I wish you well."

I heard my father attempt to backtrack and my mother yelling at him from across the house, and I hung up the phone. I cried so much because I always felt so distant from my parents, my mother especially. She and I had never had a loving moment together that wasn't fraught with the fear of death, of entering a deep conversation about things that truly mattered, or of some other impending, looming catastrophe on the horizon. My father, on the other hand, often tried to show affection in too-large of doses. I had two extremes as parents and what I desperately needed was a balance between them.

After the call I knew I had to make my move. I had nothing but Charlie and a few bags of stuff. I gave myself a deadline, stuck to it, and began making arrangements that would take Charlie and I across the country to a place I hoped would be my saving grace. I looked at it as a fresh start and knew it was going to be a life-changer for me.

I recalled the time when I was in San Francisco on tour with Soulforce. It was the most accepting place I'd ever been to in my life. I knew that somehow I would make it there okay. I heard that an old teacher of mine, Orion, had moved there and was getting his doctorate degree in Psychology. It didn't hurt that I also had a bit of a crush on him. If everything turned out, I could find a place to live, and see if this was the guy Judy was talking about years ago. I had nothing to lose and looked at the opportunity to drive across the country as a great adventure. I found a ride online and began my trek to the west coast in a small sedan with Charlie, a Chinese doctoral student in computer engineering named Wei, and a few hundred dollars I'd saved for food, lodging, and gas.

Welcome Home

I settled into a temporary sublet in the Richmond district of San Francisco (SF) with two roommates and a friend from the Equality Ride. I had the converted dining room of a three-floor home and life couldn't have been better. The trip across the country was remarkable, and my car buddy, Wei, was a great companion. Charlie rode in the backseat as our lookout and loved jumping into lakes and smelling fields along our drive.

After about a month in SF, I noticed a small mark on my leg. It looked like a pimple, so I didn't mess with it. I tried to let nature take its course, and I took care of it as I would any minor skin issue. All the while, I was on the go at my new job at an established restaurant in the Warf. Something was different though. The reddish circle around the small white center started to grow, inch by inch, per day. I chalked it up to the stress of moving and working double shifts, but nothing I tried seemed to help.

Early one morning, a few hours past midnight, I awoke with a burning sensation on my right thigh. I threw off my comforter to see what was causing such an incredible amount of pain. The circumference of the red circle had turned beet red and was now the size of a bread plate. I tried to get up, but I could hardly walk.

I made an appointment at a health clinic near Haight Street. I figured a clinic in that neighborhood had likely seen its fair share of medical anomalies.

I hobbled to the office and finally saw a doctor who took one look at me and said, "I don't know what it is, but you need to go to the emergency room. Right now." I told him I wasn't in a financial position to do so.

Noticing my meager clothes and overworked demeanor, he offered, "You're lucky you live in San Francisco. You qualify for free healthcare. Go talk to the woman at the front desk. She should be able to assist you. Go now."

I was registered with the city in a matter of moments and given public transportation instructions to go directly to San Francisco General Hospital.

At the hospital, I was greeted by a busy but gentle receptionist, checked in and waited patiently. My leg was swelling so badly it started shaking uncontrollably. When I saw the doctor, they didn't know what it was, but they knew they had to act fast, so they quickly lanced it. Without going into the gory details, let's just say they made a very painful incision, drained the wound, and placed a piece of cloth on the inside so that it would not close too soon.

They finished the surgery and I was left with a prescription for strong antibiotics. The pain was hot and throbbing; the kind of pain that you know deep down is going to take a lot of time to go away, and the only thing you can do is sit and wait. It felt like I had just been stabbed and the knife was still stuck in my leg. Every step triggered my nervous system into overdrive, and I learned how to walk with a protective limp.

Still, I had no idea what I had. No one gave me any straight answers; they would rather cut me open and send me on my way. But I thought the whole ordeal was over. So, I went on with my life and began the healing process.

I continued to work through the pain, took care of Charlie, and did my best to have a social life when possible. My sublet was nearing its end when I suddenly noticed I had another bump that looked oddly similar. This time it was on my right buttock. Every time I sat it was excruciating! No one understood what I was dealing with. I couldn't explain it because I didn't have any answers, so I just kept going and working through the pain.

This time I was more cautious. I did some research to see what it could be. I found articles online and had some talks with friends and the few family members I kept in contact with, who just so happened to be a nurse. I had a sneaking suspicion that it could be MRSA, but not many people knew much about it except for the fact that it was highly contagious.

I made my second surgical appointment and inquired about MRSA with the hospital staff. The doctor dismissed it, explaining that I did not fit the qualifications of detection and quickly lanced the wound anyway as his colleague had done the month prior. He prescribed me two rounds of even heavier antibiotics and I went home again in intense pain. When another lesion popped up a few days later, I knew something was drastically wrong. I made an appointment for a third surgery and demanded they test me for MRSA.

As I waited for the test results I started thinking. There was something I was not connecting to that no one around me was noticing. I made up my mind that it had to be something like MRSA, and I began treating it as such. I started intense research and decided to follow the recommendations of people who had had the disease. Most of the information was unavailable in conventional medical journals or online materials authorized by the medical associations. The stories of these individuals on alternative websites, however, were truly astounding. These folks were healing themselves and much of the medical community was deeply in the dark.

They could not test the wound itself as it was still subcutaneous, but they did do a nasal swab. The nasal swab came back negative. The doctor and nurses said it wasn't MRSA and that I basically had to live with it. I decided to swallow my pride and go home knowing I'd be back again so that they could take a sample and prove to me without the shadow of a doubt that I wasn't crazy.

After reading up on what I could do to treat the disease, I completely overhauled my diet. I ate all alkaline foods: greens for breakfast, lunch, and dinner. My sublet was up, and I found a lovely place in the Marina district at the last minute with an old cat lady who was an avid pot smoker. The following months would prove disastrous for both Charlie and me. I had the third surgery and the doctors finally agreed to test the wound.

I noticed that my new diet was causing the wounds to subside. The lanced areas were beginning to feel slight relief, as I continued to stay on a very strict regimen, like a raw vegan diet with daily meditations and journaling. But I needed additional evidence, so I continued to lessen my sugar intake and to cut out any form of acidic foods including animal proteins and processed foods. I even found that eating fruits and honey kept the wounds stable but cutting them out shrank them by an astonishing degree. I continued to take the best care of myself and throughout the process began figuring out ways to heal the organ I was neglecting: my heart.

Whatever was going on with me was causing me to take extra special care of myself, not just physically. I started dreaming of creating my own healing modality that could hopefully benefit people one day. I joined the San Francisco Gay Men's Chorus, sang solos at a local Unity Church, and helped a friend start a nonprofit spiritual community of which I became the President of the board. Things were looking up, but at home things were a different story.

As my health got better, I started noticing strange things going on around me. My clothes were rummaged through and my mail was left opened and out of their envelopes. I'd come home to find cigarette burns and marijuana buds on my bed, the window open and the lights left on, which was something I would never do. I'd receive calls at work from concerned neighbors that Charlie was roaming around the neighborhood off leash and unsupervised. I was pretty pissed.

I'd come home between shifts at the restaurant and find creative ways to keep what little privacy I had. I found it odd that I was paying this older woman on disability in cash each month but was smart enough to demand a receipt every time. She'd let shifty dudes with backpacks into the apartment to discuss drug deals and began allowing her ex-roommate (who apparently was a kleptomaniac) back into the apartment he was kicked out of months prior. After careful deliberation, I felt it was time to exit…stage left.

I finally got a call from the doctor's office. They told me my test results from the wound came back positive for MRSA. I looked down at my legs and noticed the scar where my first wound used to be. I had recently gotten my last lancing out and the medical team was surprised by my results but were still not convinced that it had anything to do with my new regimen. After explaining I had taken all the antibiotics they prescribed with zero effect after the first round, they chalked up my success to being young and healthy.

They believed there had to be a logical explanation and food, supplements, and spirituality was not it. They didn't want to hear about my story, even though I felt it could help people in my position who were losing hope in their care. They said there was no scientific evidence and therefore they were not interested in hearing anything further. Again, I was unable to expose the simpler truths of diseases like MRSA to the medical community.

I had begun the search for a new place and finally received a call from a man named Lee who referenced the Princess Bride in his advertisement. I knew I had hit the jackpot. I put a great deal of faith in the possibility of him calling and was shocked to receive an email from him a day or two later. I switched from working at Alioto's dining room upstairs to the more casual café downstairs. It had better hours, and I could take better care of Charlie too. I got a spare second to call Lee back on my break by the dock outside the restaurant and he invited me to stop by the following evening. I was on cloud nine and knew the end was in sight.

At work, a curmudgeon bartender tried to get me fired for "smelling like a hospital" on account of the homemade chemotherapy I was on at the time. After explaining myself, the manager let it slide because he felt sorry for me, which I was grateful for. It was the first time in a few months that I started to see the effects my regimen was beginning to have on others. For so long I kept it a secret and now it was about to cost me my job. I started relaxing a bit from my daily regimen of supplements but did not want to fully give up my healthy eating habits. I felt that it was the only thing I could do to ensure my survival and I couldn't let it go so quickly. I had to slowly wean myself off the belief that I was going to fall back into sickness.

You must understand something. I grew up sick. I spent many formative years being told my cancer would come back and that I had to do everything in my power to not let that happen. No kid wants to go through something like that--let alone twice--so I learned how to live a life that I wouldn't regret losing if I did.

This time, it was different. I was now in control of my life and I was living it on my own terms. I had to find that delicate balance between belief and reality and not lose sight of the unseen. So many people disavowed what I knew intuitively, and it got to the point that the only person who I was going to listen to was myself. Everyone else could essentially go fuck themselves.

I was about to turn 31 in a few days, and I was celebrating many months of clean living. I was happy, albeit alone, but never *really* alone. I was living with Lee and my new housemates in the Ingleside district and began work at an LGBT nonprofit in the Financial district. Things seemed on the up and up when I received a call from my friend, Caroline, from elementary school who was in town.

In school Caroline was a bubbly, vivacious girl who loved coffee and ballet. We ended up going from elementary school to college together, weaving in and out of each other's lives at various times. She asked me to come to an ice cream shop in Hayes Valley. She had a friend with her, and it would be great to hang out. I surprisingly had the weekend off, so I hopped on MUNI for what I thought was a girls' afternoon rendezvous.

When I arrived, I was surprised to see that her "friend" was a guy. The way she was talking about him, I assumed I'd be having an afternoon girls-only date. We made our way over to "Smitten" and I ordered a cup of mint chocolate chip ice-cream. They ripped fresh mint leaves off stems and poured cream into metal containers. Then, liquid nitrogen was introduced into the delicate mixture creating the instantaneous ice cream that I slowly savored with a neon-yellow mini spoon.

I noticed Bryan, Caroline's friend, was helping a group of girls with their i-Phones and I said under my breath, "What a nice guy." He seemed so content to help people with their technology, an area I'd learn later that he had a penchant for. I started thinking about my future husband and what Judy had told me. I said to myself, "I want a guy like that. I just want a nice guy." Then I looked back at him and realized he was probably straight, so Caroline and I continued our conversation about accessories.

When Bryan approached, we started talking, and he turned out to be a nice techie from North Carolina. I was excited to meet someone else who lived in San Francisco who was also from North Carolina. He had moved to the city from Raleigh several months prior, and I noticed how easy it was to talk to him. We all continued to wander through the city, and I noticed he and I continued sharing similarities along the way. It honestly shocked me how similar we were and yet how wildly different.

It took a few hours, but he invited me to a gay bar down the street to meet one of his friends, Sam. They both went straight to the bar, while I lagged behind. I asked if they were maybe a couple and they both laughed. It took me a while, but I finally realized that all three of us were gay and single. I saw the evening in a totally different light. I ended up staying at Bryan's that evening because of the instant connection I felt we had.

Months rolled by, and the more I got to know Bryan, the more everything started making sense. I began to see him as more than just a friend, but he had very recently come out and was not ready for a relationship. It was shocking to me how easy the entire process of getting to know him was. Of course, there were still moments when I questioned what I was doing with him--like when he'd want to go out drinking and watching GoGo boys all night in the Castro and completely forget about me. I would wander off and take the next train home. He'd call, flustered, and I'd explain to him that if he was interested in my company that he would need to make a bit more effort to enjoy it. After a few nights of that, I think he had more than his fair share to think about.

You see, I wasn't interested in the status quo. Going out all night and drinking didn't really appeal to me. Plus, I couldn't really do that stuff because I was scared to get sick again. There were so many issues with my health that it made even the most basic of decisions challenging.

"Chicken or steak?"

"...grass, please."

We continued our courtship, had our growing pains, and I knew that if it was what it felt like it was becoming that we'd eventually figure it out in time. I knew I didn't have to try to be anything other than what I was with him then. I wasn't going to sacrifice myself for anyone that didn't have my best interests involved and was continually surprised when he'd come back more understanding than before.

I think the thing I most appreciated about him was that he was willing to work hard for the things he believed in. It was something I hadn't ever experienced in that manner before. When it came to people, I didn't want to force anyone to do anything. I'd had enough of that in my last relationship. If someone did not want to be in my life, then I would understand. I wasn't trying to be manipulative or malicious, but it was the only way I knew how to demonstrate that I loved them: to let them go if necessary. I always believed that people who were meant to be in your life would do so when the time was right. I wasn't interested in tempting fate. I was interested in setting my sails, directing the wind as best as I could, and learning how to effectively adjust my sails accordingly.

My approach to life confused Bryan. He wanted answers; solid, tangible evidence always. The facts were paramount and if he couldn't see it, it simply didn't exist. He was extremely practical and abhorred anything remotely resembling religion or superstition. It was the first real source of conflict between us besides his fascination with GoGo boys.

I was happy but I didn't know it fully. I was still figuring things out and seeing if in fact this what was it felt like it was. I understood that when Bryan and I met we were on two very different trajectories. I was still under the assumption that Orion, my teacher friend from New York, was supposed to be my future husband. I had a crush on him that lasted several years, but I never told him about it. So I thought I'd test the waters. I wrote him an email one day and told him everything. He never responded. It was closure enough for me.

Five months rolled by with Bryan and I felt very much in love. The love between us grew from a friendship that was almost too precious. There were moments when we'd exist in each other's arms and time absolutely stood still. There was a kindred spirit there that I knew was something remarkable. I finally felt like all those couples I'd seen before: when you looked at them, they looked like they'd last forever.

On one of our nightly FaceTime calls, I asked him.

"So, Bryan, what are we?"

"What are we what?" he asked with a gentle upper lip.

"Well, we do a lot of the same stuff couples do and I don't really feel like we're just friends..."

"And..."

"And I want to know what you think of us."

He looked at me with puppy dog eyes and said, "Well what do you think we are?"

I rolled my eyes, amused that I again am left being the aggressive one when it came to intimacy and plainly said, "Are we boyfriends?"

To which he replied, "Yeah. I can live with that."

Love in the Motherland

Approaching my first anniversary living in San Francisco, things were looking up. My younger brother contacted me to say that he missed me. It was the first time in a year anyone from my family had reached out. He messaged me on Facebook with a link to the song "Daniel" from Elton John. I nearly lost my marbles.

I learned something very profound. There are times in people's lives when they need distance and space. There was so much needless suffering going on in my family that in my mind there was no other healthy option than to just let everyone and everything go. I had done my best for thirty years and I needed a major break. It took my younger brother having the courage to show me how he felt about me--of course without saying it because that's not his style--to see how important family is. There was still much more to work through, but at least it was a start. An arrangement was made to travel down to North Carolina to visit them all for the holidays. Since Bryan was from Raleigh, I thought it was a perfect opportunity for us both.

We landed at RDU and I rented a car to head straight to Bryan's family's house. It was surprising to find out that our parents' homes were a stone's throw away from each other. Thirty years of living in Raleigh and Bryan and I had never run into each other. His family was so welcoming. It was a very different pace of living than what I was used to, but Southern hospitality was alive and well. Bryan came from a traditional family where birth order was respected, hard work was expected, and family was top priority. I innately welcomed this structure and that's exactly what I got.

The moment I had been both dreading and hoping for was about to occur. It had been a year since I'd spoken to my parents and my older brother had been doing some major work on himself and on the family. He had gotten my parents to start taking better care of themselves and was doing his best to inject a certain level of consciousness to the group that I had not witnessed before. It was certainly a start, and I was able to appreciate their willingness as more authentic than ever before.

My time away from my family had helped me tremendously. I was so clearly intent on healing myself that I finally focused on taking care of the person I had become instead of trying to fix other people in the process. It was my destiny to have made the move across the country and to settle in a place that was so accepting in so many ways. I had hoped my family could have been with me on my journey that year, but it was just not in the cards. And that had to be ok.

After the holidays and getting to meet a few other relatives on Bryan's mom's side, I was sure this was a family I'd be happy to grow with. There was a very sincere, grounded love that held them together that was perhaps due in large part to the passing of Bryan's grandfather, Doc. Although he had been gone for a few years, the family mourned and honored his memory respectfully. Doc was a great man who came from a long line of doctors in their small mountain town. Bryan's grandmother, Nunner, knowingly carried the torch for her children and her children's children. I was blessed to be part of both the hilarity and the meaningfulness of their holidays that year. Bryan and I left the South and headed back to the west coast to continue our journey together.

Over the course of the next several months, Bryan and I continued to grow together. We had some tough conversations, but nothing to the extent of what I'd experienced in the past. We both were dedicated to making things work and were genuinely interested in seeing where things would go. He ended up moving in with me after a year and a half of relative bliss.

There were times when I had to pinch myself. Nothing was perfect, but I knew I was exactly where I was supposed to be. It took a whole heck of a lot to get me there, but I was finally able to be myself. I was working at a nuclear disarmament nonprofit dedicated to peace and security and that was exactly what I was experiencing in practically every are of my life.

Three years in San Francisco and two years together with Bryan was fast approaching. He and I decided to take a trip to Ireland for our anniversary and for my birthday. I'd always wanted to go but was never able to. We found a fantastic deal online that we couldn't pass up. I arranged everything with my extended family and we booked our tickets straight away. It would be Bryan's first time traveling internationally, so we planned to stay in Dublin with his work friend and then travel the countryside to see my relatives in Cork and Kerry.

At the time, Ireland was days away from a popular vote on marriage equality. We could sense a buzz around that was hopefully going to make shockwaves around the world if the measure passed. We met up with a friend of mine from my last job who lived in Ireland and was working on speaking to citizens on the grassroots level about the marriage debate. He was uncertain about the future of his beloved country and knew all too well what was at stake. Bryan and I convinced him not to give up hope, that eventually humanity swings in favor of change. It's simply a matter of time.

My cousin and his wife, who was very much pregnant at the time, bought us two VIP tickets to the Ring of Kerry tour after booking two nights for us in a beautiful hotel in the city of Killarney. It was the most spectacular tour we'd ever been on and Killarney was just breathtaking. Their beautiful son, Aron, was born a week later.

Bryan was dreadfully sick the whole trip. He downed about 12 hot whiskeys over the span of six days. One evening when I couldn't sleep, I went downstairs to the bar. I was craving something with Bailey's and my indecisiveness was irking the bartender who knew his evening was likely going to end around four in the morning. He was also pulling double duty as the concierge, which I thought was a testament to his hardworking-Irish ethic. For some reason, it felt oddly comfortable knowing the man who was guarding the hotel was also pouring our drinks.

I took my Bailey's on ice and my Bailey's hot chocolate to one of the seats by the fireplace. The wood crackled and the conversations were lively for 1 a.m. The majority of those around me were above fifty years old. It was explained to me that there was a retiree conference in the building that was taking a tour to watch the horse races there in Killarney the next morning. It's almost all I heard about for a good thirty minutes. I sat content to not know anyone and to enjoy the slight differentiations in their regional dialects.

Suddenly, a woman named Annie waltzed her way over to me. She was a spry woman in her 70's and she appeared to know everyone in the room. Well, everyone in the room knew her was more like it. She confidently asked me bold questions to get to know me a bit better and we instantly became friends. She jostled me back and forth and upon hearing that I had a boyfriend, she listened and quickly shifted gears.

"Yah noh, Dahnee, listen no. Uhy hwunt yah tah noh dat uhy ehm gonna voht noh at dee elections."

"Oh, for Marriage Equality," I presumed?

"Yes. Ehm, noh. Uhy, well, uhy jost behleev det eh marrig shoot be between wuhn mahn ehn wuhn wohmun, yah noh? It's nuttin' parsenol."

To which I replied: "Well, I'm sure it's personal to those who can't get married, but you have your right to believe what you wish. Here's the challenge though. You can already get married. Why would you want to withhold that from other people?"

She shooshed my hands from talking too loud and uttered, "Dahnee, yah noh, muhy let hoozbund's nehm hwuz Dahnee."

"Oh, yeah, I'm sorry to hear about that."

"Yah, hwell Uhy hwuz blessed.

"And wouldn't you want others to be blessed as well?"

I had a habit of asking people questions that often threw them for a loop, even though I never meant to make anyone feel uncomfortable. But my questions were never meant in malice; I was just interested in authenticity. Often, I feel like people just reiterate what they know and never ask themselves why they feel that way.

"Uhy sahpoze."

Annie yelled to the bar for another Guinness and asked me what I was having. I looked down and barely sipped my two drinks while she was up at the bar retrieving my second round. I laughed at her joviality and wild abandon. I began to think a lot about what she was saying. It didn't deter me from having my own opinion on the matter, but I wanted to try and see life from someone else's perspective. This I loved to do very much.

When she came back, a young man from the bar started asking her about her husband. Apparently, he was a very famous politician in a small village close to Rathmore, where my great grandfather had a home and a few of my cousins live today. They conversed a bit and she began to sing. With all the confidence one could muster, she belted a ditty that demonstrated where she came from. The man countered with a song from his village. I literally thought I was in a movie. Both songs, perfectly in pitch, were melodic and as ingrained into these individual's minds as anything worth remembering. These songs were meaningful, fun and artfully raunchy. I was in Heaven! The whole bar was in an uproar and everyone started singing and the hours flew by. I was surprised we didn't wake Bryan up on the 4th floor.

With the table piled high with soiled glassware, I wondered how long I'd been gone and if I would be able to speak with an American accent again. I had had so much fun I barely looked at my phone, but four hours had passed by while I was blissfully sharing life with Annie and her friends. She told me stories of all the many wonderful things she and her husband did over the years and how blessed she was to be so old, so free, and with so much money. I was still taken aback by the physical flexibility she demonstrated to one of her male suitors by pulling her shoe to her face and kissing her slippered foot. And I continued to be impressed by the power of a healthy dose of alcohol through the veins and the libido of several elderly people within close proximity.

When it was all done, Annie, whispered to me, "Uhy hohp yah dohnt tink uhy dohnt sahport yah, buht uhy hev muhy behleefs ehn dats dat. Yuhr eh goot boy, Dahnee, ehn uhy hwish yah uhl dah best!" And with that she was gone flanking down another villager who she hadn't seen in a spell.

I walked back up to the hotel room and found Bryan fast asleep. I snuck into the bed and tried not to wake him. He'd been coughing up a storm, nonstop, so I hoped he'd sleep through the night this time. The next morning we woke up and enjoyed a complimentary Irish breakfast in the lobby restaurant. I hoped I could introduce Bryan to Annie but thought she would be sleeping in on account of the late night we all had. But it appeared I was mistaken.

Annie and her posse waltzed to a table and continued their bantering session like college students. It was truly a sight to see. When we were done, we had about fifteen minutes until our tour, but I thought it was enough time to say hello before we said goodbye. I walked up to the table and met Annie's eyes. She was surprised to see me, but she quickly said, "Dahnee. Top oh thah marnin'!"

"Top of the morning, Annie. I trust you slept well?"

"Yah, eht hwuz lohfleh."

"Good. I wanted to introduce you to Bryan. I told him about how much fun we had last night and that I had hoped to say goodbye to you before we left. I hope you don't mind."

She looked a little nervous, so I thanked her for showing me a wonderful time and that I'd never forget it. She tilted her head with eyes that had likely never seen an American gay couple before. There was much less oppression where we came from in California, so I wanted to both thank her and to give her a glimpse of the possibilities that could exist for Ireland if the popular vote passed. Bryan and I walked down the steps and out the door holding hands. Regardless of the vote, I knew that Annie and I would both be thinking about each other.

On the Ring of Kerry tour, our guide had a fantastic sense of humor and a thick Irish brogue. As we travelled along the road, I recalled the trips my family made up and down the east coast to visit relatives, my trek across the Midwest with the Equality Ride, and my move to the west coast by car from New York City. The scenery now was greener and simpler but seeing the trees and the roadways pass quickly out of sight in the blink of an eye was all hypnotizing. There was a big part of me that was so grateful to be where I was, and even more grateful to have experienced all I had up until that moment.

I started to cry but having Bryan's arm around mine in the warmth of our cushioned seats was enough to keep the tears at bay. He looked into my eyes and there was no sense of reservation--nothing more to prove or to hide. It was refreshing and it assured me I wouldn't have to be alone on my journey anymore. I was beginning to get used to feeling loved in a way that made sense and just felt right. I kissed him on the cheek and watched him bashfully smile.

We stopped off at a handful of marvelous places: a historic farm, a shepherd's pasture, shops to buy each of our mothers a Christmas gift, and beautiful vistas to watch the clouds in the sky. At one spot, Bryan and I got out and he looked a bit nervous. I took his hand and showed him to the perfect spot for a picture. We smiled brightly and clicked a few until we got just the right one. I went down to grab a stone from the ground so I wouldn't forget being there, when I saw Bryan tying his shoelaces. His back was facing me, and his face was toward the bus that was waiting patiently for a few stragglers. I noticed that no one was around us and asked Bryan to hurry so we wouldn't be left behind when he grabbed my hand from his shoulder. He took my arm in both hands and traced his way to my fingertips.

"I wanted to wait until I knew you were right," he said bluntly.

"Right about what?" I asked inquisitively.

He looked at me with the kind of eyes I'd only seen in my dreams. There wasn't an ounce of pain behind them. He was certain we were right about something.

It would take him a few weeks, but Bryan ended up proposing to me when we got back to San Francisco. He bought the ring I texted him a picture of that I saw in an antique shop. It was the most perfect ring I'd ever seen and was oddly my perfect size, which was completely rare. It was gold, had etched grooves in it like scars, and in one of the grooves were five diamonds in a row. I'd never seen anything so beautiful.

"You've given me the most incredible two years of my life. I never thought loving someone like this was possible, but you continue to prove me wrong…every day."

"I hear you. I'm here with you. And It's going to be okay."

Those were the three phrases I asked him to say to me when I was feeling overwhelmed. It was the perfect thing to say at the time because it's all I ever wanted to hear from someone who professed that they truly loved me. He was my prince, my big dork, and my unbelievably stubborn Capricorn.

I took another look at him and realized nothing drastic was going to change in that instance. I didn't have to be anyone else for anyone else anymore, and the only thing I had to do was to continue to love myself and to share that love with others as much as possible. I loved him so deeply that each time I thought about him I'd feel excitement rather than pain. That's when I knew I didn't have to be sad to feel love any longer. I wanted to find happiness and there we were sharing it with each other for two full years. There wasn't a doubt in my mind that this was the right man for me.

With the wind wrestling my remaining sprigs of hair, I capriciously responded, "Of course I'll marry you, kiddo! Now, let's eat. I'm starving."

My Resurrection Story

As I look back on the last eight years with Bryan, I can say that things haven't always been easy, but life is far more rewarding in a family who cares about each other than one that's always at war. The lineage Bryan comes from is long and steady. Mostly mountain kin, Bryan's lineage is filled with a deep tradition of community service and hard-working, successful people. It's been such a blessing getting to know and love my in-laws, which can be a rarity for a lot of people. But after surviving in a family that was anything but a family, it's good to know where you stand.

It was Easter Sunday of 2021, and the voice of Tony Bennett's "The Best is Yet to Come" was reverberating from the living room speakers at Bryan's aunt and uncle's house in Jefferson. I was staying in the mountains of North Carolina, while I recouped from four years in an intense doctoral program and to finish a book that I'd been working on for the last several decades. I had just taken a nap in the guest bedroom and decided that this was the best time for me to get to work and finally arrange all my journal writings into one cohesive manuscript.

Looking over the pages of my big, leather-bound journal, I recalled times when I didn't fully understand my place in the world and why I felt so odd with who I was and where I was. I looked out the windows of the side room next to the kitchen, where I was glancing over stacks of papers and doodlings. I noticed the expanse of family land that lay before me in the quaint, yet magnificent mountain town. A place where I never thought I'd get to but where I gratefully found myself for the next two months.

Daisy and Bentley, the family dogs, were huddled next to me hoping to get yet another treat after fistfuls from kind and attentive family members. Eventually they both found a place to rest on the red sofa a few feet from the highchairs where I was perched enjoying the breathtaking sunset and picturesque vistas. A few cars came and went from view as families finished up their Easter dinners together in exchange for a sorely needed hug and person-to-person contact.

The dreaded coronavirus lockdowns had already been in place for well over a year, and I hadn't had the opportunity to shake anyone's hand until just a few days prior. People were starting to reclaim their lives again after trying to "do the right thing" and self-quarantine for what was supposed to be only a few weeks. I was lucky enough to attend church service with the family that morning and was just happy enough to spend time with people I hadn't seen since two past Christmases. I heard it had snowed a few days earlier there, but the weather was gorgeous, the birds were chirping, and the sunset was looming off in the distance.

My in-laws had gone to their cabin to check on a few things, so I was left with the voice of Tony Bennett and his friends singing duets to two ferocious love-muffins barking at people driving golf carts up the hills. I almost felt like I was attending a far-off concert from a time that was way back in our history, when people were free to roam around unmasked, yet it was oddly perfect for the quiet and serene surroundings. The lights were dimmed and made triangle shapes on the pastel-colored walls the accentuated well-framed oil paintings of country vistas and children playing in the woods before they lost their innocence. There were several chairs around me at the dining room table that were vacant but only a few hours prior sat a loving family who all told stories of the good ol' days, luckily not forgotten.

This was a time for me to relish nature and to witness the glory of God in physical form. I'd been running around the world and wanted to finally hang my hat somewhere that wasn't so chaotic and fast-paced. I never thought I'd be where I ended up and really wanted to soak up all the beauty and safety that the mountains provided me.

The sound of construction was heard off in the distance, which felt like miles away compared to the constant development that occurred daily right next to our home in Sacramento. We had moved there from San Francisco so that we could be a little farther away from the rat race. Bryan still held it against me because he didn't really want to move, but I couldn't take the city anymore. It was causing me a lot of psychosomatic illnesses and unhealthy compulsions.

Early that day, the family and I attended church at a local Methodist church and heard from a wonderful pastor about the resurrection story. It got me thinking that I never really had the time to write down what happened that day I was hit by a taxi and how this event ended up impacting my life literally and figuratively.

It took me going through an intensive doctoral program in psychology to finally be able to introspect enough to put two-and-two together regarding my near-death experience and the out-of-body experience that occurred in my twenties. I suppose it was fitting that I got to explain it all now, back home in the state where I grew up, where I found healing, and where I ended up marrying the man that I love.

I had just finished teaching a yoga lesson that morning near Trump Towers on the West Side to a client who was helping me earn money to purchase my dog, Charlie, from a kennel on the Upper East Side of New York City. I had a strange premonition that I was going to have one day a white, male, Labrador named Charlie. So I asked around to local shops to be on the lookout in case they ever received any from breeders. When I got the call out of the blue one day, I raced over to find Charlie asleep in the back of the pet shop with his sisters.

He was extremely expensive for me, but I just knew he was going to be my baby. I was working double shifts at the time to pay for him, but it still wasn't enough. My client agreed to pay for a few weeks of yoga sessions up front so that I could purchase him sooner. It was not only a pleasure to teach her each morning before work, but I was also indebted to her for helping me acquire my boy, whom I would spend the next 14 years of life with.

After finishing our session, I proceeded to walk back to the East Side on 33rd Street. I always stopped at crosswalks and looked both ways like a good boy, but this time it was a little different. At the intersection of 33rd and Park Avenue there is a tunnel that comes out to a surface road. The walk sign had just turned white for pedestrians to cross, so I stepped one foot onto the road a split-second ahead of the other pedestrians that were behind me. I made it just a few feet when there was a sudden and deadly impact.

Now at this point in the story, time and space either completely stood still or I was in some other kind of parallel universe, because it's hard to describe what I experienced in human terms. What I was unaware of at the time was that the taxi had tried to beat the red light and drove straight into my left calf, propelling my body on top of the hood of the car, where my lower back smashed through the windshield, and my body was hurled through the air onto the concrete by the impact. This may sound perfectly understandable and could be perceived to have taken a matter of seconds, but that was not my experience whatsoever.

During my out-of-body experience, I realized that I had flung head-first into the concrete and there was literally nothing I could do to stop anything that was transpiring. I was completely helpless to every single motion of the event, so I did the best and only thing that came naturally to me at the time…and simply surrendered. This was more than likely my saving grace.

During this experience, a lot of my life flashed before me. I could see, as if in slow-motion, strobe lights, a flipbook animation of each process of impact with pinpoint accuracy. Now, my consciousness could have been perceived to have been almost split. I knew something had happened, and there was nothing I could really do about it, but there was this pure bliss that took over my experience where I didn't care about any of the "reality" of it all because I was so incredibly in a state of unadulterated contentment.

What I'll never forget was that the same man that I felt standing next to me during my near-death experience in the hospital when I was five was there with me during this car accident too. I didn't make the connection until more than three decades later. But once I did, it hit me like a ton of bricks…no pun intended. I had expressed to many individuals at the hospital after the crash that I felt a man scoop me up, carry me in his arms, and lay me down on the ground as gently and effortlessly as possible. Of course, like nothing I'd ever experienced here on Earth before. I was just in a state of pure bliss.

Upon impact, I felt a man with big, safe arms pick me up, carry me through the air, and place me on the ground, as if I was a loved child. This may sound strange, given the frightening reality of what the onlookers were experiencing at the time, but it is honestly what I experienced the entire time during the event.

As I lay in this man's arms for what felt like an eternity, I felt completely protected and safe against the gentle fibers of his pillowy garment. I heard no sounds during this experience and saw no sights that were negative to me in any way. Everything at the time made perfect, absolute sense. It was just like when I was standing next to him at the hospital all those years ago. Each moment in his arms was a blessing and I had not a care in the world.

Again, I knew not to look back for some reason. I never saw the taxi behind me, but the woman who came running up to help me said that the front of the car was completely smashed in. A few other people ran up to me and said that I must be in shock because I wasn't lying dead in the street as they were expecting me to be. No, in fact I had gotten up from sliding down the pavement of the street head-first. When my body had regained its composure, I got up as quickly as I could at the time and sat in the median of Park Avenue in lotus position. Yes, I know how silly that sounds, but it's true.

I sat there in a yoga pose in the median of Park Avenue at 33rd Street, with blood spewing out of my forehead, and was in complete and utter bliss.

The folks around me tried to ask questions, "Are you in shock? He must be in shock. Someone better call the police right now!"

I answered all their questions in almost a Yoda-like fashion. Everything that came out of my lips was simple, serene, and unmoved.

"No, I'm not in shock," I'd answer each good Samaritan.

"What's your name? Where do you live? How can I help you?"

"My name is Dan. I live in Harlem. I am not in shock."

Suddenly, a Black woman pushed her way through the crowd and like any true New Yorker laid into me about getting hit by a taxi.

"Don't chu White boys know not to step into traffic like that? Serves you right!"

The woman who was helping me at the time was completely dumbfounded at this woman's callousness and didn't know how to shut her up. So the woman who was helping me dedicated most of her energy to making sure I was alright and not listening to the other woman.

"Don't listen to her. We called the police and they are seconds away with an ambulance."

When the policewoman arrived, the Black woman was telling her what a stupid White boy I was, but the woman who was helping me was torn between defending me against allegations and making sure she was applying enough pressure to my forehead. It was such a chaotic scene, but it truly didn't bother me one bit. I had just been in the arms of someone that defied all rational thought. I cannot say for certain who it was, but I have an idea of who it could have been. I knew something much larger had taken place that was given to me for my own soul's comprehension.

I couldn't believe what had happened. I felt like I was in another world. I was completely cognizant of everything around me, but those few brief moments I was flying through the air with my savior was another indication that there is something much more real about our world than meets the eye. And because this was the second time this had happened to me I no longer questioned this this fact.

How could I have experienced the same man carry me in his arms on two separate occasions? How did I just know it was the same person? I just knew; there is no other way to explain it. How could I explain what had happened to me to other people--especially to New Yorkers who eat people like me for breakfast--and would they ever believe me? The gravity of the situation was almost too much to comprehend at twenty-five years of age. That's why it took so many more life experiences and an intense psychological program in transpersonal phenomena to help me bring these experiences to the forefront.

At the hospital after the crash, the female doctor took one look at my face and did her best not to wince. She spent the next few hours talking to me and picking out shards of glass from my skin. She was delicate and precise.

She asked me a lot of questions to make sure I was ok and when she asked me about what happened, I didn't know what to tell her. So, I told her the truth as best as I possibly could. She would stop picking glass and listen to me with a shocked look on her face, shake her head in disbelief, then go back to her work with an "Uhuh" and a "Hmm..."

My paternal uncle got the hospital, took one look at me, and started laughing uncontrollably. Apparently, my father's family had a knack for laughing during uncomfortable situations and their family used to make fun of each other all the time. It was both a New York thing (ball-breaking), but also a dysfunctional family thing as well.

The second female doctor was responsible for putting the finishing touches on my care. She checked me out, asked me to do all the necessary reflex tests, and examined my forehead. Afterwards she said, "Ok, Mr. Seda. It looks like you will only need one stitch on your forehead and you should be good to go."

I was shocked because it had taken the other doctor a few hours to pick all the glass out of my face. And the worry on her told a very different story. She stitched me up, gave me some pain medication, and I was out of the hospital in time to sleep the rest of the evening.

When I woke up, I saw that the giant bruise on my lower back was strangely subsiding. Just after the accident, I had a huge purple cummerbund shape on my lower back from the impact. Now, the only thing I felt that was physically off about me was a slight nerve tinge in my lower left calf, but there was hardly a scratch left on me at all. This was just another indication that what I had experienced was seriously otherworldly.

There was no way I should have survived that accident. The amount of time my head scraped down the street, the amount of blood pouring out of my head was just inconceivable to me. The fact that the front of the taxi was massively dented in and the front windshield completely smashed in was strange enough. But the huge bruise on my lower back was almost gone and I had not broken any bones or sprained any ligaments during an otherwise catastrophic impact. This was simply too much for me to believe.

The taxi company did end up paying for my medical expenses, which was good on their part. I never did see those good Samaritans again, but I can only hope to send them my appreciation every time I think about what happened. I was so lucky to have survived the accident, but even luckier to have had one more moment with my eternal protector. Some believe it was God, or a guardian angel, and others know it was Jesus. Still some people think it was all just a figment of my imagination. But I know what I felt and I'm smart enough to know what's real and what's not real. I know what I experienced. And one day, in the distant future, I'll see my savior again.

Dying for Forgiveness

I was around forty when my mother passed away. We hadn't spoken in several years. Ever since a family text thread where she accused me of lying about a deeply personal matter that occurred when I was very young.

My mother was always suspicious of me, but that wasn't out of the ordinary for someone like her. She was a very repressed person who was not very open with other people. She didn't have any friends for as long as I knew her, and our relationship growing up was not the healthiest.

I was a sensitive kid, and I could always feel my mother's pain, even though she hardly spoke about it in any conducive way. It got to a point where I couldn't stand being around her because she made me feel like the whole room was being sucked into a vacuum. She was never satisfied, and she always assumed the worst was about to happen.

What she was never able to articulate to me was that she too was intuitive. We both got that ability from her mother's side of the family. The only problem was that my mother used her intuition to think of the worst possible things that could occur and never thought of anything positive happening. It was almost as if this natural tendency stemmed from her challenging life growing up in the Bronx with a POW father who later died of Alzheimer's, a neurotic mother who always wanted people to take care of her, and a deeply troubled older brother whom we were rarely allowed to talk about.

My uncle Bill worked as a taxi driver, lived in New York City and was in the process of getting evicted before he passed away due to the hordes of cats he had in his tiny, rented apartment. From the few stories I heard about him growing up, he as a very intelligent man, but suffered from schizophrenia, which made growing up in tenement housing in a family of six to be virtually impossible to endure.

My mother was smart. She was a woman who learned how to be tough to survive and felt as though she was not treated well by the men in her life. My mother's younger siblings, Steve and Patty, were polar opposites. Steve was emotionally repressed, and Patty was constantly craving attention. Both had their own ways of dealing with their shared childhood traumas.

The thing that hurt the most about my mother was that I was the only one of her boys who could feel her pain and tried everything to help her but was always dismissed because from her biologically minded standpoint, I was just another male who would end up hurting her. I wanted so desperately to have a healthy relationship with her, but every time I'd begin to share my experiences, she'd clench the armchair she was sitting in and the room began to feel like it was tightening in on me the more I spoke. I learned that I wasn't welcome at home, so I learned how to find ways to deal with my issues elsewhere; to find others who would give me the attention I was lacking from the one person who should have understood me better…the woman who gave me life.

What she couldn't see was that she was passing her own issues onto me and never once stopped to recognize it. She was the child of an absent father and a narcissistic mother. She had to be the parent to her siblings at a young age because her older brother was not capable of being an appropriate role model. She fought hard to make it in New York City until she found a way to escape. All of this I ended up reliving for her in my own life and she could never fully appreciate my struggles or my triumphs.

The day she died I got an email from my father, who I hadn't heard anything from since he carelessly responded to an email of mine that sent daggers through my heart. I hadn't told anyone what I experienced at the hands of my father, except my mother. She always thought I was lying, which made matters worse. I was quite innocent at the time and tried to communicate a problem I was having at a very young age with her, in the hopes that she could provide me some assistance. But that was not a feasible option.

My mother and I were in the old camper van, and I was sitting in the passenger seat in the tall comfortable chair looking out the window. I got quiet and decided to tell my mother what was on my mind and heart. I told my mother that my father was touching me inappropriately. I tried to tell her that it made me feel very uncomfortable, so that maybe she could help to stop it, or at least make sense of it for me because I was too young to know any better. In my heart, I knew that what I was experiencing was not good, so I was reaching out to her for help and guidance.

Months prior, my father, my younger brother, and I were sitting in the oversized brown armchair in the den at the Plateau Lane house. Erik and I were young and in our underwear. I must have been maybe six or so and he must have been about three years old. I remember a hand tickling my testicles and going inside my pants. I had felt his hands go quite low in the inside waist part of my pants before, but this time it had reached my gentiles in a way that felt less like tickling and more like something else.

He was always kissing us too much, squeezing us too tightly, and rubbing my legs too far up my thighs. I often felt suffocated by his hugs that lasted way too long and always made me feel uncomfortable. The part that I really had a hard time with was that he used to kiss us on our cheeks with his tongue. It was so strange and all I wanted to do was squirm away from him, which was odd for an otherwise affectionate kid like me.

After he touched me in my underwear, he quickly turned me around to face him, and shook me violently. He shook me with both of his strong hands on my tiny upper arms so aggressively that I felt like I was a bowl of jelly. He looked at me dead in the eyes and said, "Don't you ever let anyone ever do that to you. You hear me! Don't let anyone ever do that to you!"

I was so confused. I didn't know what to do except to tell him, "okay." My voice was meek and perplexed. My father was so angry, and I watched his anger subside only after figuring out how to change the subject. I sat there on his lap for what felt like ages and I can't remember what happened after that. I was just glad that he hadn't reached that point with my younger brother, as far as I could tell.

Now here's where things get complicated. You see, I really don't hold anything against my dad for his wandering hands. I used to, but I was able to make peace with it by staying as far away as possible. I understand he may have had his own issues because I heard stories about my male cousin on my dad's side molesting his younger sister at night for years. I only heard about this when I was in my mid-thirties, so I carried a lot of excess weight on my shoulders for a very long time thinking that somehow--yet again--I was at fault for something that was out of my control. Dad may have taken advantage of a situation that I'm sure had playful undertones, but the overly affectionate behavior continued, which was deeply confusing and upsetting to me.

I told my mom in the car about the incident as best I could because the situation was eating away at me and I didn't see any way of stopping it. I didn't want my younger brother to have to experience that. Even then, I was doing everything I could to think of other people ahead of my own needs, which was not healthy or sustainable.

My mother stopped the car in the parking lot of our old elementary school. She pointed her fingers at me and said, "You watch too much TV, Danny. Don't ever tell anyone about that ever again." She made sure I knew never to talk about the situation again, which I didn't, until I was in my early thirties and in therapy. Unfortunately, the second time I called on my mother for assistance a few months later, she reacted in the same manner.

When my father was around he used to hold my little brother and I's hand at night while reading us a bedtime story. My father was much more of an improviser than my mother, who wouldn't be caught dead reading a book to us for any great length of time. His stories were usually adaptions of nursery rhymes that had explosive sounds in them to add more action to keep a boy's attention.

One time, he was in my bed and was going too far like usual. I felt like he was going to suffocate me into the pillow; I couldn't breathe. He was kissing me on my face with his tongue and I kept trying to cover my face from him. At that point, I was somehow successful at stopping him, and he turned his attention to my younger brother.

All I could hear was tickling and uncomfortable laughing, which was usually how the behavior started. However, this time it was different. I began to hear my younger brother wince, which deeply affected me. I could feel him at this point because I knew what that felt like. So, after the third wince, I just couldn't take it anymore. I was about to burst when I saw my mother walk out of her room and pass our doorway, only a few steps down the hallway.

I yelled for her and said, "Mom, help! Dad's kissing Erik with his tongue."

She stopped and stood cold in the doorframe. She glared at me, then at my father. My father got up from Erik's bed and said, "Annie, Annie! He's just a kid. He doesn't know what he's talking about."

At that point, my mother glared back at me, turned her back from the doorway, and headed right down the hall, clear out of sight. I was completely dumbstruck. I couldn't look away from the hallway in hopes that she'd come back and somehow make everything better, but that was the first time I remember being completely devastated. I was too scared of what my father was going to do to me, so I sank back into my bed, pulled my covers over my head, and prayed to God that I would disappear. I was paralyzed by fear and complete abandonment.

That was the second time I desperately needed my mother to help me handle such a sticky situation and she simply refused. She thought I was a liar and that perspective never left her. From that point on, I knew what it was like to be utterly alone in the world, and to be considered the epitome of hatred in a mother's eyes. There was nothing I could do to win back her approval no matter how many awards, trophies, and scholarships I would earn. This demonization for telling the truth plagued me my entire life.

So cut to decades later just before our wedding. During a heated text thread, my mother referred to the time I told her about what I was experiencing as a young child in front of my whole family and wrote "...Just like you lied about your father doing all those horrible things to you."

I responded, "I think it's best that you don't attend our wedding. I've received better mothering from others in my life and you can't hurt me anymore."

At that point the conversation in my eyes was over, but not for the rest of them. Both Erik and my mother had to have the last words and wrote, "Exit stage left, Danny." Another blow making fun of my chosen profession at the time. No matter how much blood, sweat, and tears I poured out on stage to bring my full self to my work, it was always seen as another opportunity for Dan to lie to people. This was too much for me to bare any longer, and so my husband and I decided to close shop with the Sedas and move on with our lives. Luckily, I was basically adopted by my husband's family, who were incredibly family-centered and compassionate people.

At the funeral, I managed the music for the ceremony. My aunt Patty provided fake, plastic flowers because she knew that this would be what my mother would have wanted. Fake flowers were the only flowers my mother let my father buy her while they were married. I got to conduct a small choir of my friends and sang a few solos at the event, which was nice. I also recited a eulogy that I hoped would offer peace and closure to my family in our time of need.

I felt it was appropriate to find a way to overcome all the drama now that my mother was in a far better place. I always knew that she'd be a better parent after her passing because then at least she'd be able to meet the man who saved my life and leave all her animosity behind. At this point, I didn't hold any more heartache because I knew she was in a place where she knew better and was able to see things in a clearer light than she ever could before. It was never about any of the small stuff, but about the larger picture, which can allude the best of us when we haven't had the intimate experiences of life and death as often as others have.

I took one look out into the crowd and saw my younger brother with his boatload of children and wives and my extended family (some of which I was still in contact with, and others not so much). My husband didn't want to attend the funeral because to him Annie had caused too much turmoil for the both of us. That was hard for me, but I had to respect his wishes. This decision made me stronger because I didn't have any of my husband's physical strength there to lean on. I had to find it within myself. Plus I was a bit too afraid of what he would do if he saw my family. It would be awful if he ended up going to jail because he let his temper get the best of him in a delicate situation.

My mother's body rested in her casket but her soul, of course, was elsewhere. I couldn't look at the body for too long because I was afraid that she was going to come back to life and yet again make me feel like I was the worst person in the world. I could feel the stares and judgements of the other family members as I passed the coffin on my way to the stage. I tried to find old friends of hers to attend the funeral but there was no one to be found. My father, of course, couldn't stop crying. He would bawl loudly during speeches and it got to a point where it was becoming a real issue. But I had to keep my mouth shut and be as respectful of everyone's process.

My older brother, the recluse, kept to himself per usual. He was now the only uncle that the nieces and nephews had since I'd fallen out of the family's graces. This was a strange fact for me to comprehend, since throughout my life, Mike was an unbelievably destructive sociopath. It was my hope that his Christian conversion in his early thirties would teach him a thing or two about rectifying his past misgivings. But I was not the beneficiary of Mike's inner work. I hoped that his nieces and nephews were. That at least would provide me some respite for the future.

I took the microphone in my hands and asked my cousin, Alicia, who was my "best woman" at our wedding, to stand by me in case my younger brother (the sheriff) and his second wife (a police officer) decided to abuse their power to keep me from speaking at the funeral. I took a deep breath and began to utter the words that I'd painstakingly typed out on a few clean pieces of recycled paper:

> *We often find ourselves in situations that can appear never-ending; whether one subsumes a totality of responsibility or an absence of such to save face. I never knew my mother and it appeared from her words and actions that she never knew me. I know that she loved me as best she could, given what little she had to grow from. I always knew we'd find a way to reconnect when her walls were eventually torn down by something she couldn't control. Sometimes, it takes a tsunami for someone to reveal themselves; their pain and strength bobbing on the surface of the water like lost luggage or sinking further into the abyss deep within the heart of the ocean. My mother was not an easy person to love. She was a complicated, victim of circumstances; practically everything I did my very best not to be but would fail at from time to time. I often wished I had a mother who I could have been best friends with. I wished I had a mother who I could talk about everything under the sun with, or who wanted to have spa dates together and talk about what was weighing on each of our hearts and minds. Someone who wanted to see me find love beyond the limits of their own critical judgements. For much of my life I felt so utterly alone. I had to depend on myself to find my own answers, which in retrospect could have been a blessing in disguise. I wonder what she's experiencing now. I wonder who she's standing next to and who she's been able to bare her heart and soul to; someone who could listen to her and offer her the perfect words of wisdom that she could never find here on Earth.*

I wonder if she's finally experienced the love we all deserve to have that can be so precious and fleeting during our Earthly incarnations. It is my hope that she has found what she had been searching for her whole life. It is my sincere wish that she understands now who she was meant to be beyond the circumstances she may have found herself in, along with the rest of us. I long to see her happy and at peace for the first time. Aside from the clenched jaw avoiding a broken-toothed smile, beneath the thick-rimmed glasses that hid her beautiful face, and beyond the grey hairs that she never did anything with besides pull back with a dollar store headband. She was everything I did everything I could not to be until I got married and saw parts of her in me that I didn't like. I saw her rigidity, her withholding affection because she couldn't muster it for herself, and the desperate attempts to employ control over her temper when the men in her life were behaving like men often do. I understood her in ways she could never know, and I got tired of trying to prove my worth to her, so I left. I left a younger brother I loved and helped raise because I didn't know how to stay. I left an older brother who I couldn't reach and was too scared to help save. I left a father I hardly knew because I couldn't accept his unwillingness to change. I left a mother who may have loved me but was never able to show it in ways that nourished my heart and soul. I wished things could have been so very different for us all. I wished I could have saved the world somehow without killing myself first. I wished I could have been a better uncle, and brother, and son under kinder circumstances. I wished I could have been a more easygoing person, but that was not what God and life had created me to be. But now I know what she's experiencing up there. I know because I experienced it here. I know she's witnessing the same hands that held me before I came into this world, the same hands that taught me to look at the reality of my existence to decide whether to stay or to go, and the same hands that held me close to His chest when I was in utter peril. Just like my father's hands who answered my call to pull me out of turbulent waters when I was drowning as a child. Just like the rough hands of my mother's father for whom she shared a similar grasp. She's with our Father now in Heaven looking down on us and sending us all love. The love she may not have been able to fully express here with the limitations each of us possess. Now, she's with us in a manner that will bless all our lives in ways we may not be aware of just yet. She is able now to give us all what we need to help us carry on with our missions here on Earth. Missions that if we already achieved would render our lives obsolete. We still have work to do, and I know that now she's only a thought and a heartbeat away. I pray she's recognized who she truly is and finds ways to help each of us reveal who we really are amidst the chaos of a very mad world. I pray that each of you recognize your own divine spark before your unique light is extinguished. I pray that you live a life that respects creation yet releases the need to fear the unknown. I pray that you all honor your individual paths and find ways to support others along your journeys. I pray that if you need someone to guide you that you know who to call upon. I pray that one day when we all meet again that it is in a place where we can finally see each other in the light of our truest form, the one that God had originally designed us to be and who we still are behind the veil of separation. I know that we will see Annemarie again, but until then we have more work to do here. In closing, I'd like to say that I forgive you, Mom. And I now know that you have forgiven me too. In Christ's name we pray. Amen.

Heaven Help Us!
A monologue by…Dan Seda

God...listen up! (*Lights up*). I'm a lawyer! I make six figures and I have a twenty-year-old mistress in Staten Island. You can't just uproot my entire existence in one fell swoop. (*God speaks*) I never said you said, "Heaven was democratic." (*The man uses the entire stage as if it was a courtroom*) I mean, look at this place. Everything's stark white and smells like antiseptic hand soap. If anything this place is reminiscent of a staunch, communist dictatorship, rather than a democracy, and further more...(*God speaks, the man is startled*)...Well, fine. I am just saying that....(*Whining*)...well this sucks! (*Coming to terms with the situation*) Fine, how did it happen? How did I die? (*God answers*) Oh, come on, I live in Brooklyn. I don't even own a chainsaw. How could I have...(*God smiles*)...Oh, ha, ha, ha. Very funny. (*Talking to a few people behind him in line*) So, God's got a sense of humor, huh? Okay, I'll let that one slide. Listen. (*Pauses, looks around, something catches his attention*) You know, God…may I call you God? (*God shrugs*) Thanks. You know, if you brought a few real estate investors and a construction team of illegal immigrants up here, you could really whip this place into shape in no time. I mean look at the square footage, (*Facing upstage*) AND THE VIEW! (*Coming downstage to face God again*) Not to mention, all you'd save on overhead. (*God speaks*) What? (*He listens*) I know. (Saddened) Okay. (Angry) But, why? (Explosive) WHY DID I HAVE TO DIE? (*Trying to prove his case he, in the process, gets gradually lighter in tone*) I was doing really well for myself. I had my own Mercedes. A summer home in the Hamptons. I even had one of those Jack LaLane juicer things my wife made me buy. She saw it on some infomercial one night. It's a long story. The doctor said I needed to eat more fruits and vegetables on account of my… (*God speaks. The man answers admittedly with a heavy, Brooklyn accent*) Yeah, well, it's my cholesterol, you know? (*Internal realization*) Well, you would know. (*Trying to avoid*) I blame it on the fast-food industry. (Side thought) Have you ever seen that movie *Super...*(*God speaks as the man trails off in thought*)*...Size Me*? What? (*God repeats Himself*) You're gonna what? (*Surprised*) I didn't even know we were allowed to do that. (*Intrigued*) Okay. (*Trying to hear God over loud music booming out of car speakers*) What's that? I'm sorry. (*God continues*) No, it's all that loud music coming from that jerk's sound system! (*Speaking toward off-stage*) HEY, BUDDY! (*Stomps his feet*) WOULD YOU SHUT UP ALREADY, WITH THE '*BRINGIN' SEXY BACK*' SONG FOR CRYIN' OUT LOUD? I'M TALKIN' TO GOD HERE. (*Calming down and bringing his attention back to God*) Sorry God, what were you saying? (*Loud music pipes in again*) Hold that thought. (*Resumes his argument with the jerk*) Yeah, I know he's talented, but come on. The whole idea of bringing something back that never left to begin with is ludicrous. Alright? (*Flamboyantly gay*) It's Sss-imply ludicrous-sss! (*Slaps his mouth shut. He stops straight and looks at his hands in disbelief*) Dude, that was so gay. (*Facing God*) Did you make me do that? That wasn't me just then. (*God speaks. He answers.*) No, it wasn't. (*Angry and uncomfortable*) NO, IT MOST CERTAINLY WASN'T! (*God speaks forcibly. The man backs down immediately in fear*) Okay, okay, fine. Your house, your rules, you win. (*Mumbles*) You happy now? (*The man walks around contemplating his escape but stops noticing God is knitting something on His sofa*) God, is that...are you macraméing a potholder? (*God answers*) Rrrriiight. (*God speaks*) Oh, it's a scarf! Well, that just clears up everything...whu, why are you macra...nevermind. I'd like to discuss something with you...(*God gets up and walks over to His kitchen*) Wha...what are you doing now? (*The man finally sees what God is doing and speaks in disbelief*) Are you making spinach dip in a sourdough bread bowl? (*Notices where he is and speaking to anyone who will hear him*) Who's having a dinner party in the middle of a snowstorm? This is Heaven for Christ's sake! (*Christ appears with a tie-die shirt and a ukulele waving "Hello." The man quickly speaks to Christ as if everything is* *chill*) Sup, Jesus! (*Christ disappears in a flash*) What the Hell? (*The floor opens up and the fires of Hell can be seen below*) Ahh! (*He jumps back, stops, looks at God*) God you are really starting to freak me out here. (*God is in the living room about to put on an exercise DVD*) No. No! NO! Put down the Taebo DVD and get back on your throne! I'm trying to have a divinely intelligent discussion with you about the purpose of life. (*Whining*) Come on man, this is serious. (*God makes his way over to the CD player and suggests some music. Tired, as if from a long day in the courtroom, the man says without realizing.*) No, now for the last time, I don't wanna listen to Barbara Streisand! (*Out of character and flamboyantly gay*) It's sssoooo cliché. Now would you...(*Realizing what just happened he intensely whispers*)…Oh, my God. (*Long pause*) God? (*Pause*) Are you gay? (*Quickly*) I don't wanna know. I don't wanna know. "Don't Ask, Don't Tell," I firmly adhere to that. (*He looks around for some help or some semblance of reality. He can't find it anywhere and is markedly uncomfortable. Trying to change the subject he offers*) I think my WIFE would love the number to your decorator...this place is pre-tty suh-weet. (*God speaks*) My mistake. You do exceptional work, my friend. (*Stops fighting*) So, what is it you want me to do with my life this time? (*He listens and protests*) Oh, no. No, no, no I can't do that. You want ME to be... Ha! I mean, come on… I didn't agree to this a few moments ago when you said I had another chance to go...(*God puts His hand up in and turns His gaze away. The man revolts*) Oh, yeah? Who says so, huh? Who says? (*God silences him*) Okay, fine…but you can't do that. You can't make me gay. It's not fair! (*God speaks*) OH, COME ON! I hate showtunes! (*The man rants and raves around the stage*) I read the sports section! I walk around my house in week-old boxers drinking orange juice out of the carton. I piss on the toilet seat when I urinate. On purpose. It's a ritual. (*God asks*) I don't know why? It's just easier, I guess. (*Begins to ask tentatively, then works up the courage to ask God*) Why do we have to die? (*God pauses and answers*) Hey, that's not fair! You can't use **my** answer to answer **your** question. That's not how this works. (*The man finally gets it. He begins to speak more candidly*) Ok. What am I gonna do, what am I gonna be when I grow up? (*God answers*) Great. How typical: a gay, music teacher. Well, that's just PERFECT! (*Angry*) What, are you gonna strap little bells on my shoes and make me drive a SAAB to work? (*God answers*) I'm gonna ride a bike? A bicycle? (*Sarcastically*) With a little horn and a wicker basket for Toto too? (*God speaks*) I'm sorry, I couldn't hear you. What was that? (*He reiterates what he hears unbelievably annoyed*) 'Because I'm afraid the carbon monoxide pollutants in the air may be contributing to the catastrophic effects of global warming?' Let me get this STRAIGHT? Ok? So I'm gonna be a tree-hugging, helmet-wearing, baton-twirling…(*He stops midsentence to answer God who was interrupting*) Oh, yeah I got it. (*Angry as Hell*) BULLSHIT! NO WAY, MAN! OUT OF THE QUESTION. (*Flying off the handle*) For crying out loud, how can I...(*To himself*)...where do I go from here? (*Back to addressing God*) There are no limits to the humorous undertones one could take with what you're telling me here. I mean really. (*Realizing God's not laughing, the man suddenly sinks a bit*) And you're not laughing. (*The man uncomfortably tries to make light of the situation*) Come on, I thought God had a sense of humor, huh? (*God speaks. The man mocks Him with his best Charlton Heston*) "Not when it comes to my planet and my children." My God, God, you sound so biblical. (*Long pause*) That's another thing. Did you literally write the Bible? I mean are those really your words and nothing, but your words so help you...You? (*God speaks*) Okay. (*Becoming clearer, the audience sees a noticeable change take place in his character toward vulnerable sincerity. He takes a deep breath and begins*) Well, you better tell everyone else that. Because you've got a lot of folks out there believing it is and they're condemning a whole bunch of innocent people with their fearful misperceptions. (*Relieved, he speaks to himself*) Did I just say that? It felt pretty good. You're not mad at me for saying that are you? (*God smiles*) Hmmph! (*Introspecting and complete energy shift*) You know maybe this idea of giving it one more shot isn't so bad after all. There are far worse things than being an eco-friendly, bicycle-riding, rubber-horn-honking, gay, music teacher…(God adds and the man finishes)…with impeccable hygiene. You mentioned that before. I know. I was listening. (*Upbeat*) Well, okay then. I guess I'll pick up my halo at the front office. Yeah, your receptionist is lovely by the way. I didn't get a chance to thank her before when I was.... You've been very kind and this whole "experience" has been rather quite enjoyable! (*He begins to walk away, forgets and, then remembers smacking himself on the forehead*) **Oh, God**...Sorry. Hey, do I have to wear product in my hair and really tight jeans? I mean I just hate it when my package gets all bunched up. No. (*God gestures him to leave*) Okay, thanks. I'll just...(*The man points to the door and heads upstage. He turns around again before forgetting, genuinely intrigued*)...do these halos come in different colors? Cause you know if I'm gonna…(*Limps wrist in the air*)…I might as well learn to…(*Poses flamboyantly*)… ACCESSORIZE! (*Laughing and very light-hearted*) Okay, alright. This is gonna be fun! Thanks, God. (Starts to leave and *remembers*) Oh, and God…I love you. I just...wanted to say that before…(*The man pauses before exiting, afraid to finish his sentence. He beings to walk away when God speaks. The man stops to face God and listens*) Yeah. I know. (*The man exits. Lights out.*)

--- THE END ---

Made in the USA
Las Vegas, NV
11 May 2021